NEW DIRECTIONS FOR PROGRAM EVALUATION
A Publication of the American Evaluation Association

Nick L. Smith, *Syracuse University*
EDITOR-IN-CHIEF

Minority Issues in Program Evaluation

Anna-Marie Madison
University of North Texas

EDITOR

Number 53, Spring 1992

JOSSEY-BASS PUBLISHERS
San Francisco

MINORITY ISSUES IN PROGRAM EVALUATION
Anna-Marie Madison (ed.)
New Directions for Program Evaluation, no. 53
Nick L. Smith, Editor-in-Chief

Microfilm copies of issues and articles are available in 16mm and 35mm,
as well as microfiche in 105mm, through University Microfilms Inc., 300
North Zeeb Road, Ann Arbor, Michigan 48106.

LC 85-644749   ISSN 0164-7989   ISBN 1-55542-759-6

NEW DIRECTIONS FOR PROGRAM EVALUATION is part of The Jossey-Bass
Education Series and is published quarterly by Jossey-Bass Inc., Publishers (publication number USPS 449-050).

EDITORIAL CORRESPONDENCE should be sent to the Editor-in-Chief,
Nick L. Smith, School of Education, Syracuse University, 330 Huntington
Hall, Syracuse, New York 13244-2340.

CONTENTS

EDITOR'S NOTES

This volume is based on the premises that the goal of redistributive policy is to address social and economic inequities in means-based opportunities and that one of the roles of the evaluator is to determine whether social policies and programs have attained this desired outcome. This volume constitutes a new direction in program evaluation in that it links methodological, moral, and ethical evaluation issues to the minorities who have the highest stake in the attainment of social policy and program goals.

Although racial and ethnic minorities and poor people are disproportionately among the intended beneficiaries of redistributive policy, they have little input into defining social goals or interpreting the impact of social policy on their lives. The fundamental question is not whether the evaluation enterprise is capable of determining the truth about the outcomes of social programs in the lives of individuals designated as the beneficiaries of redistributive social policy; rather, the question is whether evaluators are willing to employ the greatest range of techniques in the discovery of the truth. The contention is that discovery of truth must entail mechanisms for input from the populations most directly affected by social policy.

It is generally acknowledged that evaluators and the minority populations that are overrepresented as beneficiaries of social policy are, for the most part, dichotomous groups. These groups differ culturally, socially, and economically, yet people affected by the programs evaluated depend on evaluators to validate the degree to which desired social outcomes are achieved. In this relationship, evaluators are in a position of power in that their critical judgments and interpretations of the truth about the relative quality of social programs may have serious consequences for the lives of minorities.

Placed in this context, evaluators must view themselves as more than technicians. They are discoverers of truth as it concerns the goal of achieving a just society. First, evaluators have both an ethical and a moral obligation to examine the efficacy of existing evaluation technologies in determining the impact of social programs on the lives of the poor and minorities. Second, evaluators should seek alternative strategies that can provide more balance in the discovery of truth by incorporating the world views of the minority groups that participate in social programs. Third, evaluators should be concerned about whether issues of social justice are addressed in social policy and programs. Such issues are those that are fundamentally embedded in the majority-minority imbalance in the distribution of power and resources and in the social outcomes of this imbalance.

There may be several reasons why only a few evaluators have addressed the human issues of concern to minorities, such as social justice (Sirotnik, 1990), cultural dominance (Lincoln, 1991), and the political consequences of evaluation (Guba and Lincoln, 1989). Questions about whether redistributive policies and programs are substantive or symbolic are largely ignored by evaluators. Ericson (1990) points out that one of the reasons for this omission is that "evaluators generally disclaim any responsibility for judging the ends or aims of the programs and the institutions that design and implement them" (p. 6). This disclaimer allows evaluators to insulate themselves from the social justice issues that are important to minorities. Another reason may be that, in the quest to validate evaluation as a legitimate form of scientific inquiry, evaluators have been reluctant to address these issues because of the perception that such questions may threaten the field's scientific validity. In this quest, evaluators have not acknowledged that evaluation is fundamentally a human enterprise (Sirotnik, 1990).

The aim of this volume is to begin discussion of some minority concerns about the impact of cultural dominance on definitions of social goals and on the measurement of their outcomes in a culturally diverse society, and about the political consequences for minorities of cultural dominance in the selection of evaluation methods. This volume also offers techniques and procedures for including minorities in the evaluation process. These techniques and procedures may enable more accurate assessment of social conditions, of the programs that address social conditions, and of interpretations of social programs' and policies' outcomes.

Each chapter of this volume presents an evaluation issue that has consequences for minorities. The first two chapters report evaluations in which the individuals who were to benefit from the programs were included in the evaluation process. The authors of these chapters report their experiences in the application of various techniques for understanding the world of the program-targeted population.

In Chapter One, Michael Baizerman and Donald Compton identify some of the problems inherent in using conventional evaluation methods to determine the outcome of educational programs. They report observations from ongoing evaluation research on educational reform policy in Texas. Their primary focus is the impact of the policy on minority youth and adults who were the targets. The authors illustrate the usefulness of including minority parents, students, and educators to help the evaluator understand how the policies have actually worked in their lives. The roles of parents and students as informants, respondents, consultants, and participants are described as ways for the evaluator to put into practice the moral basis of his or her work—learning the truths of others.

In Chapter Two, Stacey Hueftle Stockdill, Rose Marie Duhon-Sells, Ruth Anne Olson, and Michael Quinn Patton discuss empowerment of ethnic minorities to act in their own interests. A multicultural educational program was implemented in five minority communities by a multicultural team of evaluators, program staff persons, and community persons. The authors present a process for program development and evaluation that can empower a community to design a program on the basis of the objectives of the community that the program is to serve. The process provides an opportunity for a community to design a program representative of its world view by defining its own concerns and the appropriate strategies for addressing them. The authors challenge readers to become involved in such a process and to share in learning about it as they experience it.

Chapter Three, by Anna-Marie Madison, summarizes the basic minority issues in program evaluation and makes the transition to the more technical concerns addressed in the three chapters that follow. This chapter explores the potential for developing programs and evaluations that incorporate racial and ethnic minorities into the evaluation experience. The author advocates primary inclusion of targeted minority populations in all aspects of program development and evaluation and raises questions about the adequacy of current evaluation methodologies to discover truths about program development, implementation, and outcomes.

In Chapter Four, Ceasar L. McDowell discusses the punitive effects of assessment methodologies on minorities. The author examines the effects of cultural bias in testing and documents the extent to which reliance on standardized tests as the only assessment tool may detract from important programs designed to offset inequities in means-based opportunities for ethnic and racial minorities. Testing bias has been an issue in educational assessment for the last three decades, but McDowell raises new questions that involve interactions among culture, cognition, language, social capital, and testing and the consequence of these interactions for minorities.

Chapter Five, by James Earl Davis, discusses race as a variable in evaluations. Davis examines the limitations of current evaluation models and techniques for understanding the impact of social policy on the lives of minorities. He critically examines the practice of using traditional comparative analytical methods to identify race differences in program evaluation. Davis contends that program evaluations often focus on outcomes for different racial groups but that these differences are usually identified without clear articulation of what race means in an evaluation context.

Chapter Six, by Jeffrey S. Beaudry, examines problems inherent in the evaluation of multicultural educational programs and how this issue is related to minority group's concerns. Beaudry uses a meta-analysis of the effectiveness of bilingual education to illustrate his points.

The topics presented in this volume are only a few of the many minority issues in program evaluation. Because minority-majority social and economic disparities and the concept of social justice are recent issues in the field of program evaluation, the contributors ask readers to accept the challenge of exploring this new area.

Anna-Marie Madison
Editor

References

Ericson, D. P. "Social Justice, Evaluation, and the Educational System." In K. A. Sirotnik (ed.), *Evaluation and Social Justice: Issues in Public Education.* New Directions for Program Evaluation, no. 45. San Francisco: Jossey-Bass, 1990.
Guba, E., and Lincoln, Y. S. *Fourth-Generation Evaluation.* Newbury Park, Calif.: Sage, 1989.
Lincoln, Y. S. "The Arts and Sciences of Program Evaluation." *Evaluation Practice,* 1991, *12,* 1–7.
Sirotnik, K. A. (ed.). *Evaluation and Social Justice: Issues in Public Education.* New Directions for Program Evaluation, no. 45. San Francisco: Jossey-Bass, 1990.

ANNA-MARIE MADISON is associate professor of public administration at the University of North Texas, Denton. Her work includes evaluation of a wide range of human services programs and policies, focusing most recently on evaluation of social programs for the older adult population.

Program evaluation can invite dialogue with the people affected and, in so doing, become a chorale of many voices.

From Respondent and Informant to Consultant and Participant: The Evolution of a State Agency Policy Evaluation

Michael Baizerman, Donald Compton

George Bush claims to be the "education president," and during the week of April 15, 1991, he called for a vision of public education and for the necessary reform to realize it. His was but another in a very long national history of stated visions and calls for school reform. One such recent call was made in Texas.

Texas was challenged to assess its school system by a coalition of business, political, civic, and educational leaders. In June 1983, the governor appointed the Select Committee on Public Education, whose purpose was to conduct a comprehensive study of the public educational system. Recommendations were submitted in April 1984, and in June of that year the governor called a legislative special session.

Among the recommended reforms were higher graduation requirements, passage of an exit-level competency test for graduation, a no-pass/no-play rule, and five-day absence policy. This wave of educational reform continued during the 1989 legislative session with the addition of a driver's-license bill and a modification of the attendance policy. The at-risk student population was the target of only the driver's-license bill, which was designed to keep students in school by requiring school enrollment for a driver's license to be obtained. The attendance policy, the no-pass/no-play rule, and the exit-level competency examination were designed to raise standards for all and encourage all students to give greater effort and attention to school work.

Some interpreted these policies as a more or less honest effort, however late and partial, to reduce risks for the targeted population. Others perceived these policies as a way to continue to push out from school the very children, adolescents, and youth whom schools were serving poorly. The result would be a student population ready, willing, and able to learn (and to use computers, that being the business of the committee chair, the famous industrialist H. Ross Perot).

As with most other social, public, or educational policies, there were many players involved in the creation of these, many intended audiences, and multiple possibilities for intended and unintended consequences. Indeed, given the work of Edelman (1971), the very title and language of a policy must be scrutinized, for therein lie clues to its politics and to its uses as a sociopolitical instrument. The Texas Education Agency (TEA) implemented the Select Committee ideas which became law as four policies to improve the schools (that is, the education of Texas's children and adolescents) came to be defined and responded to partly as policies for at-risk students.

In what follows, we report on an effort to use a policy evaluation to create ongoing dialogue with people who, at least through the evaluators, could tell decision makers how their everyday lives were being made different by the changes. In a preliminary, limited way, the effort succeeded. Philosophical sources and derivative practical actions are noted, as are the design, method, and selected findings of the evaluation study. This attempt is presented as both an ethical stance and a political act.

Risk: Implications for Minority Students

The TEA policies were a political-educational response to a variety of social, structural, and sociopolitical situations present nationally and, even more acutely, in Texas. These included the following:

The deep structural shifts in the state's economy away from oil, agriculture, and real estate and somewhat toward high technology

The need in high-technology industries for educated and trained labor at the entry level, as well as in the professional and technical ranks

The increasingly visible and growing underclass, a large percentage of which comprised people of color and, among them, a growing percentage whose second language was English

The growing and intrusive crime rate, with related drug problems and all the personal troubles and social issues corresponding to the nationwide rural and urban social crisis.

At moments of social structural change, Americans may feel vulnerable and, in response, may focus on the near, the psychological, and the "basic"—the family, the neighborhood, schools, and work. In any event, national and local attention was given to schools and their presumed role in economic stagnation, delinquency, adolescent pregnancy, the teaching of values, and the like. Indeed "the school," like children and like adolescence, is for Americans a metaphor of hope, possibility, and opportunity (Baizerman, 1986). Focusing on schools is a way of trying to change the larger, more abstract, more distant, less visible, and harder-to-grasp world.

Risk. The language of risk joined these personal feelings of anxiety, depression, and anger to the social realities of children and adolescents who were doing poorly and leaving school. The typical phrase was "students at risk."

Risk is a technical term in the language games (Van Peursen, 1970) of public health (MacMahon, Pugh, and Ipsen, 1960; Nelkin, 1985) and its specialties (such as epidemiology, and safety and occupational health) and in insurance, from which it migrated to the health sciences and then into education and everyday, nontechnical speech. It has long been and continues to be a term in the study of adolescence (Dryfoos, 1990). It is important to review the technical construction and use of this term in order to sensitize the reader to its ideological uses in educational policies and programs.

Technical Definition. *At risk* has a technical meaning in public health epidemiology (the study of the incidence and prevalence of disease), where, as we have just said, it was taken up from its use in the insurance industry (where it was in turn basic to the mathematics for determining liabilities and selling costs). In epidemiology, which is a form of "disease accounting" (MacMahon, Pugh, and Ipsen, 1960), *risk* refers to "those persons who are capable of having or contracting a disease" (p. 229). Persons in the population group have a certain mathematical probability of having or contracting a particular disease; thus, one can compute a population probability and an individual probability.

At risk, as a description of mathematical probability based on research, is part of the arithmetical computation known as a *rate.* To use the concept of risk scientifically, there must be empirical research showing relationships among factors. Risk is related to action—to lowering (or raising) a population's susceptibility to a particular disease. One form of action is prevention. Education took the term *risk* and the possibilities inherent in prevention and control and used these to discuss students, policies, and programs.

At Risk as an Educational Term. The technical term *at risk* has a new home in education, where it has come to have several meanings, not all of them technical in the sense of this term's use in public health. In Texas, students are identified as being at risk on the basis of such state academic criteria as test scores, retention in a grade, or status of being two or more years below grade level. School districts can identify additional students on the basis of such psychosocial variables as pregnancy or substance abuse. In many schools, this process results in the majority of students' being identified as at risk. One purpose of identifying students as at risk was to locate students to be served, but numerous studies in Texas have shown that fewer than half the students who drop out of school have been identified as at risk. This is hardly surprising, since the educational use of the term *at risk* does not meet the test of the public health definition—that is, it is not known whether the characteristics used for identification actually predict which students are most likely to drop out of school.

TEA and, more generally, the whole field of education use the concept of risk as part of an ideology, thereby joining science, mathematics, and morality. The major use of this ideology is to construct a socioeducational population of at-risk students and suggest that they are both the problem and its cause. The school is absolved and can be expected only to "do its best with limited resources." Whole schools and even districts are not thought of as being at risk; the problem and its sources are the students.

Risk and Race, Ethnicity, and Social Class. Embedded in the concept of risk as used in education are the realities of race, ethnicity, and social class, as well as those of family, neighborhood, and community. This is so because failure, dropping out, and their correlates (adolescent pregnancy, English as a second language, family status, and so on) are social facts distributed unequally across races, social classes, and ethnic groups. Minority students show higher rates in these areas, almost regardless of which population is a minority in a particular school. Very often in Texas, the minority students are students of color—Hispanic, Vietnamese, or African American, depending on the school. Hence, to talk about risk is to be heard, by some, as talking about minority youth—"them." In this sense, *risk* is a code word for *race.* Thus, to evaluate a program understood as being concerned with at-risk students is to enter the realities of race, class, and ethnicity and to discover how these show up in the lives of students and are seen in school policies, programs, and practices. Evaluation has to engage these realities; this is its moral basis.

Evaluation. The evaluation of the four policies was designed by TEA staff and funded by federal and state sources. It was to be an in-house study, typical of the many being done by TEA at any moment. The story of the evaluation, which is still in progress, lies in how the ordinary was made deeper and richer by a radical return to its roots. Part of the story is contained in the evaluation team members' backgrounds and beliefs. The team members invited those who were interviewed to use the team (among others) as spokespersons. The team also espoused certain rights:

The right of the people touched by the policies to talk about how their everyday lives were changed

The evaluators' right to learn about the issues they thought important

The right of those affected to be part of the political discourse on the policies—their purposes, strategies, implementations, and consequences

The right of the public (the community) to be informed about the policies, their political and educational meanings, and their possible impacts

The evaluators' right to allow the policies to teach them how to study the policies

The evaluators' right to tell the world what was learned, including what others wanted them to tell

The evaluators' right to teach their questions to the people they talked with, so that they would learn new ways of questioning.

Along with these rights, the evaluators also acknowledged an obligation to hear the targeted populations' questions and learn how they understood the world. This sense of the evaluators' obligation was understood in the spirit of play and joy, not as a burden. Evaluation is play, an infinite game—one that can matter. This sense of moral obligation and play led to an evaluation plan characterized by methodological diversity and to a conception of evaluation as an inherently political process.

Evaluation as a Political Process. The four policies were designed—by a highly public, highly politicized committee—to meet a highly troubling public issue, framed variously as the failure of the schools to teach or as the failure, inability, or unwillingness of students to avail themselves of the opportunity to learn and prepare themselves for a "changing world" (of work). Any evaluation of these policies would be political in that there were constituencies interested in the findings, and there were political careers (and bureaucratic careers within TEA) linked to the politics in their population focus and as strategies for change. Given the racial, social-class, and ethnic distribution of the at-risk population and the use of risk as code for race, any evaluation would also be involved in the politics of race.

In light of the seemingly conservative culture and centralized organizational and policy structures of Texas education, these four policies were thought by some to indicate a major shift in TEA's focus—to poor, minority, and troubled students, in predominantly poor schools in urban ghettos and dying rural towns. The policies were seen by some as an opportunity to work in the real issues of Texas education, issues long avoided. That the policies were visible and political only made the opportunity to work on the "real" issues more inviting, indeed seductive (especially so, given the normal range of TEA evaluation topics, approaches, and methods). It was believed that an evaluation of these policies could make a difference to Texas education and to the targeted students, who were often ignored by the schools. Evaluation was a means of "doing good."

Methodological Diversity. The multistage, multiyear evaluation was designed to be methodologically diverse so as to accomplish the several goals of assessing policy effectiveness, in classical ways as well as in the evaluators' being taught by the respondents, most of whom were students of color (as were counselors, faculty, and administrators in the schools and, often, at the district level). Since classical designs, as well as classical procedures and instruments of data collection, tend to be relatively insensitive to deep cultural and social-class differences, it was decided to use multiple methods to meet the multiple goals. Together, these show the study to be innovative.

The classical methods included the use of a sample of approximately 1,800 at-risk high school learners in fifty school districts, who were a cohort in a three-year longitudinal study. One innovation was to pay school district staff to collect data.

A statewide survey of all Texas high school principals was also conducted. The purpose of the survey was to assess the principals' perceptions of the effects of the four policies on both at-risk learners and those not at risk. (Rarely have principals been asked their opinions.)

Another component was a yearly case study of the same eight high schools. This case study included visits to each school, to interview district and school staff and faculty who were being affected by the policies in their everyday lives. Through the evaluators, they began to have a(nother) voice and to teach the evaluators about the many realities of the policies. They were invited to be consultants at each stage of the evaluation. The intention was to keep learning from them and to provide a means for their voices to be heard in the state agency, in the state board of education, and in the legislature.

Still another element was the use, with at least one class of students per case-study school, of a "youth poll," open-ended questions about the four school policies. A later addition was a non–participant-observation study in a nonsample school in another city.

The data from each component were used to understand the others, in an expanded "triangulation" of data. Also innovative was an invisible shift, in which data from each approach were used as sources of questions for all other approaches, each year and over time. Thus, the questions became deeper and richer as the evaluators learned about the policies in practice.

Most crucial was another shift: from "collecting data" from a "subject" or "respondent" to creating a "dialogue with the Other" (Buber, 1965) in the interviews, in the youth polls, and in the draft reports sent to the participants. In other words, those who were interviewed were invited to review and reflect on the "findings" and provide comments and recommendations. In this way, the evaluation became a dialogue, both during and after visits to the schools.

What Was Learned

The authors learned about risk, politics, and evaluation, and about the limits of goodwill and evaluation competence.

About Risk. At-risk students are youth—kids to themselves, and to most of the school staff. TEA-defined risk is the basis of school practice, but many staff people have their own understandings of who is really at risk, and why. The more the school and its faculty and students come from the same world, the more the school seems to operate according to real-world criteria of risk.

The concept of risk can be used variously—for, or against; in the service of, or to block or deflect. To start with the least obvious point, *risk* is a word that makes programs and services possible. Some students choose to be labeled *at risk* because they want access to services (they are clever and adept, if not good at exams).

At-risk students also constitute funding and service categories. Hence, in the school's political economy, risk is a way of getting special funds for teachers, materials, services, and consultants.

Risk can be used in the service of a moral and political account, one that legitimizes a school's failure to meet the needs and wants of certain students: "We are doing the best we can with what we have"—that is, with these resources, this kind of student, this kind of school, this type of child or adolescent.

The term *risk* is used by adults, not by students, and is used to refer to those who are not doing well, who are not likely to do better—those of whom one should expect little, those who make life as a school professional difficult. The language of risk is a language of exclusion and denunciation. To the extent that the concept of risk is thought of as overlapping social class, ethnicity, gender, neighborhood, and other social categories, it is used as a form of "cultural politics" (McLaren, 1989). *Subculture* can become *sub* culture, as in subordinate culture, as in less good—a moral evaluation. In this way, the term *at risk* can become a technical term, which in cultural and ethnic politics is used to solidify hegemonic cultural control. *Risk* can be used as a new word to allude to victims, the dispossessed, the troubled, or, in the classic phrase, to the "sick, crazy, stupid, bad, dirty, and little."

About Politics. Evaluation does and does not matter in the real world. It matters little to TEA, it matters some to the district staff, and it matters more to the school staff. The evaluators' early work was heard by the state board of education, with no apparent effect on the policies for at-risk students. Among the school staff, it was a different story: the closer to the students one gets, the more the evaluation is asked about, and the more it is used to reflect on school policies and learn from other schools.

To the extent that evaluation is a way to use one's voice to comment on something intended to influence one's world, it is part of an ongoing discourse about policy and programs in a public agency. This is politics. It can represent one voice among many and the voice of many. Evaluation can become another player in the political game.

About Evaluation. Evaluation can be political in the various ways noted, as well as in terms of group politics, elections, and the like. Evaluation can also be an infinite game, ever-evolving and ever-deepening. This is most true when one uses a dialogical perspective to transform technical activities into the possibilities that can flow from relationship, from hearing and listening, from true dialogue. Herein lies the link to voice, narrative, story, liberation, and emancipation.

Can Evaluation Really Liberate and Empower?

The potential is there for evaluation to be liberating, emancipatory, and empowering. That potential was not realized in this effort, but the evaluators did learn about how to begin to make that happen.

The simplest shift is to perceive those one wants to interview as people first, people one wants to talk with, and then as people who can teach one, and then as people one wants to spend time with and can even enjoy. These perceptual shifts prevent one from seeing people as subjects of a psychological exam or as respondents to a sociological instrument. Instead, in the language of anthropology, they come to be seen as *informants*. Then it is easier to work with them as consultants. None of this ignores them as political persons, activists, parents, or anything else. At best, they can join evaluators in true dialogue as people, not as "role incumbents."

All of this suggests that evaluation research is a political process, in a variety of senses. It is purposeful, sponsored, and implicitly or explicitly for *and* against something, if only its grand claim to "truth" or, better, to a perspective on a phenomenon (Freire and Macedo, 1987). Evaluators of educational and other human services programs tend to live in social realities different from those of program "clients," closer to those of "providers," administrators and policy makers. Educational, social-class, and social-style differences imply power differences, as does the fact that the research is sponsored—that is, given a kind of legitimacy (and simultaneous illegitimacy) and funding. If an evaluation study is a political process as well as a situational political tool, then evaluators must be very alert to the inherent power inequality between themselves and the people they want to interview.

Evaluation is also a morality, as well as a technology (see Schwandt, 1991; Sirotnik, 1990). As moral action, it can be oriented to virtues (wisdom, justice, temperance, courage) and can use them in evaluation of programs and services. In this way, morality and politics are joined.

Moral evaluators can try to understand the people they are talking with, not as social science "roles" or as "representatives" of larger "samples" but as people who speak and whose ideas can become a "voice"—a perspective on the world, and a statement about the world. Evaluators can choose to amplify this voice, using the evaluation study as one means to do so (if permission is given, of course).

Many "voices" can contribute to and become a discourse. Evaluation as a moral enterprise can be partly about the creation, sustenance, and shaping of discourses about the world. In this way, a radical return is made to a core idea of evaluation—as perspective, judgment, and advocacy.

Evaluation, *in its very process* and as a moral enterprise, can sensitize individuals to their moral right to have and use their voices and to join in constructing a discourse about their worlds. Evaluation, *in its very process,* can be an invitation to tell one's stories; this, too, is a moral right. This argument is a form of the "existential advocacy" (Gadow, 1980) now being debated in nursing and medicine (Bishop and Scudder, 1990; Mishler, 1984). By now we are surely beyond seeing evaluation and social research as simply collecting Durkheimian "factoids"; we are struggling to understand the Buberian Other (her meanings of her worlds, his places within these).

Evaluation has a deeper, richer potential: to teach its participants that they are not objects or things, and to do this by showing them one way to "read" the world. Literacy, for example, can be the skill "to read the word and to read the world" (Freire and Macedo, 1987, p. 1)—that is, literacy is a form of making sense out of printed words and lived worlds. So is evaluation. Good evaluation, in its root sense, requires a sensitized, critical consciousness and an ability to reflect. Evaluation can be a form of education and thus can teach literacy and *conscientizaçao* (Freire and Faundeg, 1989). Evaluation is educative. It is education, it is moral education, and it can be political education.

Can there be any *educational* evaluation that does not claim the moral ground and political right to educate? Evaluation of schools, curricula, services, and programs can and must be educational in that the very processes that constitute evaluation must be put into the world as ways of learning that belong to everyone; so too with the "findings" and the final and interim reports.

Evaluation can be politically democratic in its intent, in its methods, in what it does with what it learns, and in what is taught. This is not a political or ideological distortion of educational evaluation; rather, it is a radical return to its roots in the morality of social justice and caring. It simply puts *téchnē* in its place.

Evaluation and the Involvement of Minorities

How would an evaluator assess the goals of making evaluation include the perspectives and voices of Texas's minority communities and sharing with those communities what was learned about TEA's at-risk programs? Overall, the evaluation reported here would be found wanting—partially successful in learning, but relatively less effective in sharing what was learned.

The evaluators' early belief was that, since there was relatively little special effort made in most TEA evaluations to include minority voices, this aspect should be emphasized. This was a driving moral and (professionally) ethical force. At-risk youth tend to have disproportionately low participation in large surveys, but such designs and instruments are increasingly preferred by overworked TEA staff—who, in any event, come from academic cultures that are quantitatively oriented and insensitive to how such studies in themselves deflect the very input they seek. The simple fact of relatively high geographical mobility among these youth and families results in low follow-up rates (or high study-dropout or loss rates), with concomitant distortion of the findings toward more geographically stable populations.

The use of multiple data-collection methods challenged these methodologically instigated flaws while contributing to clearer, more appropriate, and more effective questions. Group interviews work well in learning the actual languages of an issue, as spoken by youth and students. To ask questions is often to stimulate interest in the answers on the part of the person who is asked. Such questions and interest can lead to reflection on the topic of the questions and to awareness about and deeper understanding of the topic or issue. This happened in all the interviews with youth and school professionals, and it was with the latter that the evaluators shared the draft and final report. Many in both groups were members of racial or ethnic minorities. How much farther into the community these people passed on their interest, concerns, and understanding is not known. Articles were sent to many Texas professional journals (for coaches and school boards, for example) but not to parent newsletters, although this surely would have helped democratize the debate. While many school staff are minority-group members, this is less true among central TEA staff people and among those who carry out and write up evaluation studies.

Democratic ideology aside, and parent and community "involvement" aside, schools are insular. While there is probably some insinuation of these ideas by minority-group school professionals into their communities, it is uncertain, as are the quality and perspective of the ideas. Little was done about this, beyond stimulating legislative and newspaper debate, which is essentially debate among and for elites. A "community variable" should have been included in the study, and the evaluators should have taken to the streets to learn what "the people" knew, believed, and wanted to tell.

What did emerge for participants in the study may be ironic: that TEA evaluations and assessments are constantly going on, and that people are unaware of most of these; that most TEA evaluations do not really matter to the participants (or perhaps to anyone) in any short-term, tangible sense; and that participants may be able to be players in evaluation, and in the other ways in which program decisions are made locally and statewide—that is, they have a story and can choose to give it voice. That was the hope of this evaluation, and this may have been its sole and limited success.

References

Baizerman, M. L. "Why a Community Needs Its Adolescents." Paper presented at the First International Meeting on Youth, Hong Kong, December 17, 1986.

Bishop, A. H., and Scudder, J. R. *The Practical, Moral, and Personal Sense of Nursing: A Phenomenological Philosophy of Practice.* Albany: State University of New York Press, 1990.

Buber, M. *The Knowledge of Man.* New York: HarperCollins, 1965.

Dryfoos, J. *Adolescents At-Risk: Prevalence and Prevention.* New York: Oxford University Press, 1990.

Edelman, M. *Politics as Symbolic Action: Mass Arousal and Quiescence.* Chicago: Markham, 1971.

Freire, P., and Faundeg, A. *Learning to Question: A Pedagogy of Liberation.* New York: Continuum, 1989.

Freire, P., and Macedo, D. *Literacy: Reading the Word of the World.* South Hadley, Mass.: Bergin and Garvey, 1987.

Gadow, S. "Existential Advocacy: Philosophical Foundation of Nursing." In S. F. Spicker and S. Gadow (eds.), *Nursing Images and Ideals.* New York: Springer, 1980.

McLaren, P. *Life in Schools: An Introduction to Critical Pedagogy in the Foundations of Education.* White Plains, N.Y.: Longman, 1989.

MacMahon, B., Pugh, T. F., and Ipsen, J. *Epidemiology.* Boston: Little, Brown, 1960.

Mishler, E. G. *The Discourse of Medicine: Dialectics of Medical Interviews.* Norwood, N.J.: Ablex, 1984.

Nelkin, D. *The Language of Risk: Conflicting Perspectives in Occupational Health.* Newbury Park, Calif.: Sage, 1985.

Schwandt, T. A. "Evaluation as Moral Critique." In C. L. Larson and H. Preskill (eds.), *Organizations in Transition: Opportunities and Challenges for Evaluation.* New Directions for Program Evaluation, no. 49. San Francisco: Jossey-Bass, 1991.

Sirotnik, K. A. (ed.). *Evaluation and Social Justice: Issues in Public Education.* New Directions for Program Evaluation, no. 45. San Francisco: Jossey-Bass, 1990.

Van Peursen, C. A. *Ludwig Wittgenstein.* New York: Dutton, 1970.

MICHAEL BAIZERMAN is a professor in the Center for Youth Development and Research, School of Social Work and Maternal Child Health, School of Public Health, University of Minnesota. He is a consultant to the ongoing study.

DONALD COMPTON was project manager of this five-year study. He is now associate evaluation specialist in the Division of Research and Evaluation, Virginia Department of Education.

*In this chapter, voices from one multicultural evaluation convey
a sense of the struggle involved in developing an evaluation that
is sensitive to and empowering of multicultural peoples and
perspectives.*

Voices in the Design and Evaluation of a Multicultural Education Program: A Developmental Approach

*Stacey Hueftle Stockdill, Rose Marie Duhon-Sells,
Ruth Anne Olson, Michael Quinn Patton*

An important new direction for program evaluation is to seek ways of actively involving people of color in evaluation processes. This means adding a multicultural perspective to stakeholder involvement processes. Stakeholders do not just represent power positions, program constituencies, and key influences. Different stakeholders also bring varied cultural perspectives to evaluation. These include differing experiences with, beliefs about, and trust in "data," research, and accountability.

The purpose of this chapter is to share some of what we have learned about involving communities of color in evaluation. The source of these lessons is evaluation of a multicultural education program.

We have come to think about multicultural perspectives in evaluation as involving different voices. The format of this article allows some of these different voices to speak about involvement in the evaluation of a multicultural education program called Supporting Diversity in Schools (SDS). The program is working to create links between community groups and schools for five minority populations in Saint Paul, Minnesota: American Indians, African Americans, Hmong, Cambodians, and Hispanics.

This chapter presents a chorus of voices on one particular multicultural evaluation. The collection of voices is not entirely cohesive, sequential, or logical. Our aim is to convey a sense of developmental struggle as we work together to create a shared evaluation process that is sensitive to and empowering of people of color and respectful of their diverse perspectives.

As a context, we offer the voices of three SDS staff members from different racial and ethnic backgrounds. They talk about their experiences with evaluators and evaluation in multicultural settings:

What has frustrated me in the ways multicultural programs have been evaluated is that the people who do the evaluation generally do not understand the nature of multicultural work. . . . The evaluators and their evaluations often miss the point of what the program is about and use inappropriate standards on which to interpret the program and on which to make value judgments. They often choose not to evaluate some things that are relevant and miss other important things altogether. My frustration is that you have to educate the evaluators before they can do reasonable work. Often I end up using their formats and instruments, even though I know they are not capable of accurately assessing the value of the program. With the new developmental approach to evalua- tion we're using in SDS, I feel very good about the process. In my opin- ion, as an African American, the process is fair. It is nonthreatening because it is participatory, and all involved have an opportunity for input. It is in line with our multicultural philosophy and the nature of multicultural work because all perspectives are allowed to come to the table and are taken into consideration [SDS coordinator].

My experience with program evaluation stems from my ten-year involve- ment in Indian education projects and programs in several school dis- tricts. During the early years of my work with Indian education, the evaluations were conducted by white evaluators who did not have an in- depth understanding of Native American cultural dynamics and charac- teristics. We learned through this process that it was difficult and uncom- fortable for Indian parents and staff to talk with evaluators. Consequently, the evaluators missed a great deal of valuable information regarding program activities and parental concerns. The evaluators did not come away with a complete and accurate understanding of the program, and the biases of the evaluators, resulting from their lack of knowledge about Native Americans, were reflected in the final product [SDS associate director].

In the federally funded multicultural programs in which I have been involved, as a Mexican American, a program officer usually comes in, and it is very cut-and-dried. You said you would do these things, and they check to see if those things are done. Some of the program officers act like "Mr. In Control" and give the impression of "I can yank your budget if I want to." The SDS developmental evaluation approach is important because the program people have the opportunity to deter- mine the parameters of the program itself, as well as the details of its evaluation. This process guarantees varied cultural perspectives. It has been difficult, in some ways, because the process is so new and because past experiences with evaluations tend to color what people think it will be about. It's hard to really believe that we, the project people, have input [SDS coordinator].

These are the voices of people of color reporting their experiences with evaluation. Now we share the voices of the people who have had primary responsibility for the SDS "developmental" evaluation process. In so doing, we provide more details about that process and the program.

A Vision for Multicultural Education and Evaluation
Rose Marie Duhon-Sells

Rose Marie Duhon-Sells is cofounder and executive chair of the National Association for Multicultural Education. She is also dean of the College of Education of Southern University, Baton Rouge, Louisiana. She has written many articles on multicultural education and is the synthesis evaluator for the SDS program. As synthesis evaluator, she is helping the program to extract lessons learned and to interpret those learnings in a national context. Duhon-Sells establishes the context for this discussion of the evaluation of SDS by briefly explaining the emergence of multicultural education as a major curriculum issue in American schools and giving her views on evaluation challenges for multicultural education.

America is in an era of transformation. Family forms have become so diverse that there is no longer a "traditional" family form. Women are more politically active. By the twenty-first century, racial and ethnic groups in many areas of the United States will probably outnumber whites for the first time. Demands for multicultural education—and therefore multicultural evaluation—arise in part from these vast demographic shifts, as well as from the accompanying political dynamics and changes in values (Grant, 1991).

The multicultural thrust will be a key element in the restructuring of the educational system in America in preparation for the twenty-first century. There is a need for a new paradigm of multicultural education at all levels—and thus a need for evaluation to be multicultural. The cultural and racial diversity of this country should be fully utilized in both education and evaluation. The richness of each ethnic group can contribute in ways that will be beneficial to all.

The federal government has spent millions of dollars on programs to effectively educate America's increasingly diverse population. While many outstanding projects have resulted, funds have also been awarded to individuals who, in retrospect, seem to have meant well but were unaware of the magnitude of the problems associated with implementation of a multicultural thrust in the curriculum. Moreover, the concept of multicultural education often has been misinterpreted by educators, and the real issues have been circumvented or ignored in search of a rationale to justify avoidance of genuinely multicultural education (Sleeter and Grant, 1988). Evaluations of these misguided efforts have contributed to the problem by failing to incorporate multicultural processes and sensitivities.

Multicultural educational programs have taken several forms and followed several fashions. Some focus on the foods, clothing, and entertainment of various cultures. Others encourage individuals of European descent to be sensitive to and tolerant of cultures different from their own. Still others seek to integrate multicultural perspectives into all aspects of the curriculum. The approaches to multicultural education are many. In my opinion, however, most multicultural education projects and approaches have failed dismally in their efforts to meet the challenges of diversity.

I believe that the major challenge is to provide an educational experience for all students that will help them learn more about themselves and others. The true historical backgrounds and major contributions of diverse cultural groups must be addressed positively in America's schools. It is to be hoped that, in studying diverse cultures, students will learn how to view the development of humanity from multiple perspectives. Effective multicultural education goes beyond understanding and acceptance of different cultures; it recognizes the right of different cultures to exist as separate and distinct entities and acknowledges their contributions to society. Effective multiethnic education helps students develop cross-cultural competence. This entails helping all students develop the attitudes, skills, and behaviors needed for effective functioning in their own ethnic groups, in American society generally, and within and across diverse ethnic groups.

Accordingly, evaluations of multicultural programs should include assessment of the extent to which students are developing multiple perspectives, appreciation of diverse cultures, and cross-cultural competence. Evaluations of multicultural education programs should also model diversity through the active involvement of people of color. The complexity of multiracial perspectives must be embedded in all levels of evaluation design and implementation.

Much remains to be done in developing and implementing effective multicultural education in America. Evaluation can best contribute to increased effectiveness by incorporating people of color and their diverse perspectives at every stage, from conceptualization and design to interpretation of findings and formulation of recommendations for program improvement.

Supporting Diversity in Schools Through Family and Community Involvement
Ruth Anne Olson

Ruth Anne Olson has had a private consulting practice in educational program design and evaluation since 1971. She has worked extensively with K–12 school

districts and with private and corporate foundations that support public educa-
tion. She is the SDS program director.

What Is SDS?

In Saint Paul, as elsewhere throughout the nation, achievement scores and
rates of enrollment in institutions of higher learning are lower for students
of color than for white students. Dropout rates for students of color are also
higher. SDS is based on the hypothesis that the racially homogeneous
professional staff of our local schools is ill equipped to address the educational needs of an increasingly heterogeneous student body and that strong
links between schools and communities of color are necessary to change
the dismal statistics.

Our mission in SDS is to reduce the educational inequities experienced by children as a result of race or culture by building school environments that welcome, appreciate, and effectively teach students of color. We
seek to accomplish this mission in the following ways: (1) helping to build
curricula and school environments that are free of cultural and racial privilege, (2) helping school staff learn from communities and families whose
cultures are different from their own, and helping them apply their new
skills and knowledge, (3) affirming and strengthening the role of community organizations as cultural bridges between schools and parents of color,
and (4) affirming families of color as needed experts and resources regarding their children and their cultures.

SDS is administered by The Saint Paul Foundation. It is funded by
The Saint Paul Foundation, the F. R. Bigelow Foundation, The Bush Foundation, the Cowles Media Foundation, the Knight Foundation, the Mardag
Foundation, The St. Paul Companies, Inc., the General Mills Foundation,
various individual donors, and in-kind support from the Saint Paul public
schools. SDS is managed by a multicultural staff that includes a program
director, an associate director, and four coordinators. A volunteer community advisory committee and a donor review board are responsible for
program policy decisions. The program began in August 1989 and will
continue through August 1995. Its six-year budget projection is approximately $2 million.

School/Community Partnerships. The SDS staff has helped forge
several partnerships between Saint Paul elementary schools and organizations that serve communities of color and established four partnership
contracts of $25,000 each for the 1991–92 school year. These contracts are
as follows:

Hmong Pride Connection: The activities of the Mississippi Elementary School
and Hmong American Partnership have included the development of
multicultural instructional materials, monthly workshops for parents and

school staff to exchange concerns and information, and miniresidencies through which Hmong artists and Mississippi Elementary School teachers will team-teach Hmong arts.

Making a Difference Is Our Business: This partnership of Maxfield Elementary School and Family Service of Greater Saint Paul focuses on African American issues and has sponsored counterracism training for parents and staff, training for community members to serve as advocates for students of color, and support for a group of target parents who seek to develop strong communication between parents and teachers.

On Eagle's Wings: Saint Paul American Indians in Unity and Jackson Elementary School have come together in partnership to implement a variety of activities, including cultural sessions to expand knowledge and pride of Indian heritage, a school pow-wow, purchase of culturally accurate materials for the school library, and a retreat for teachers, parents, children, and community members.

Sahaka Siksa Kaun Khmer: The activities of East Consolidated Elementary School, the Refugee and Immigrant Resource Center, and Merrick Community Center have included support for cultural representatives to work with teachers and children, a Cambodian New Year celebration, diversity training, and parent-teacher forums on such topics as cultural communication and school/community values.

While all four partnerships began with a focus on the culture and issues of one community of color, each will be required to include issues of additional communities in later years of implementation.

Educational Activities. SDS sponsors a variety of educational activities that are open to the public. Workshops have focused on such topics as the histories and cultures of various racial and national groups, white privilege as a barrier to pluralism, and learning styles in respect of diversity. A daylong "community plunge" encouraged teachers to become familiar with community organizations, and a multicultural book group meets monthly to discuss books from a variety of cultural perspectives.

SDS also provides incentives for educators, parents, and community organization staff members to attend theatrical performances and other events in local communities of color. Finally, the SDS staff publishes both a monthly newsletter that reports on program-related issues and events and a monthly calendar that informs readers of public activities related to local communities of color and issues of diversity.

Barriers to Communicating the Vision of SDS

The purpose of SDS has always been clear to those of us who created it: we want schools to be equally fine places for children of all races. We want them to be places where adults and children are as excited and supportive of a classmate's experience of a pow-wow as they are of childish pleasure over a birthday party, where parents are confident that their fears of racial barriers will receive unhesitating respect and action, and where every child is reflected in the literature being read, the history being examined, and the customs being recognized.

Throughout the first two years of the program, we experienced difficulties in communicating SDS's purpose. Inevitably, these problems created barriers to effective implementation and evaluation. Three overlapping dimensions contributed to communication problems: the broad range of meanings given to such words as *multicultural* and *diversity,* the differences in the perceived importance and intensity of our mission experienced by white people and people of color, and the structural barriers to adequate communication within largely white power-realities.

Words as Barriers to Communication. From the beginning, the creators of SDS struggled with choosing the words that best describe our purposes. We talked of *multicultural curriculum and instruction,* of *breaking down the isolation of schools and communities of color from one another,* and of *family involvement.* Those words and phrases brought powerful images to our minds. We quickly learned that they brought equally powerful but quite different images to the minds of others.

When people in SDS talk of *multicultural curriculum and instruction,* we mean full and complete integration of all races and cultures into curricular content, instructional processes, and all interactions related to schools. We learned the hard way that many people hear the words as meaning something quite different—special units of study, display of artifacts, multicultural fairs, and shaded faces in textbooks.

Two Views of the World. SDS was born of the hopes, dreams, and anger of people of color in Saint Paul. It is true that many white people, myself included, have "tagged along," but I know that I can touch only the surface of the urgency and agony felt by people who have *lived* these issues and become steeped in the hope for life to be different for their own children.

Many white people choose to get involved for a variety of reasons: it's the right thing to do, we are stimulated by the personal growth that results, and it's an opportunity to bring together many varied strands of the values that underlie our lives. One must always remember, however, that as a white person, involvement is a choice. For most of my colleagues and many of my friends, involvement is no choice at all—it is synonymous with living. I am convinced that it is nearly impossible to fully bridge the gap between those two realities—that it is impossible to fully communicate the mission of SDS across large numbers of people when the experiences that individuals bring to reality are so widely disparate.

The differences are visible in a thousand ways in SDS. One can hear them in the varying intensity with which people talk of what needs to be done. One can feel them in the great differences in how people interpret the realities of day-to-day interactions. One can see them in the differing body language of people listening to strong presentations about education, race, and prejudice.

Two worlds are objectively reflected in the split responses on the evaluation forms concerning many of the speakers we sponsor and the performances we host. The vast majority of our participants of color give a thumbs-up and a "right on"; large numbers of our white participants either ho-hum with "This was not new" or protest, "We addressed those issues long ago." The reality of these two worlds is a constant barrier to communication and problem solving. Trying to step from one world to the other, even for a glimpse of the differences that exist, is risky business. Honest communication falls victim to the protection that people create for themselves.

Dominance of White Institutional Power. Because of those two worlds, discussions of virtually any topic vary enormously according to the racial and cultural identities of those involved. All-white, predominantly white, predominantly "of color" and (I'm told) all "of color" groups yield tremendous variations in tone, content, and conclusions.

SDS is about racial and cultural diversity, and early on I made a promise to myself never to arrange any "official" discussion of the program that would involve an all-white group. In fact, I pledged that people of color would be in the majority in all such discussions.

I quickly discovered that I had underestimated the intensity of the problem. For example, there are times when it is important to meet with the foundation funders of SDS. Until recently, all the foundations were headed by white people. Some program issues call for frank discussion with the principals of all the schools in SDS partnerships. In the first two years of the program, all the principals were white. Evaluation issues occasionally create the need to meet with evaluation staff members in the school district—all white. Often, of course, I also need to meet with the people above me in the hierarchy of The Saint Paul Foundation. All are white. Even the heads of many of the participating community agencies that serve communities of color are white.

What this means, of course, is that the people who head organizations and make daily decisions relevant to the achievement of racial equity have little opportunity to hear the realities of their fellow citizens of color. Even more rarely do they have the opportunity to hear them in settings in which the people of color feel the confidence of expression possible only when the majority of those present have shared the daily reality of discrimination. The isolation of white people form these issues inevitably leads to our inability to learn, understand, and respond effectively.

Implications for Evaluation. Each of these barriers creates significant challenges for evaluation. Program participants must agree on the meanings of key words and concepts in order to agree on evaluation criteria. Two views of the world can constitute insuperable barriers to defining problems and programs, and white dominance cannot be allowed to shape the criteria and processes for a program grounded in diversity.

Getting Unstuck. The problem for SDS has been to figure out how to get unstuck from these issues of communication and commitment. We have worked hard at it, have made some progress, and recognize that much more effort is still needed. I believe that our attempts at solutions are worth sharing.

To address the issue of a common language, we have gone through a long and intense process to fully comprehend what we are about. A great diversity of people has been part of that process. We have tried to shy away from words that label and to focus instead on words that describe.

We are also trying several strategies to bridge the gap created by the fact that some people *live* and others only *observe* the issues of racial discrimination. We believe, for example, that the arts and humanities play a major role in the process of bridging the gap. In our multicultural book group, teachers and community people together discuss works by writers of color that bring human experience forward in all its richness. We provide incentives and encourage people to attend events: a classical Cambodian dance performance, an Indian pow-wow, an African American theater performance, and exhibits of Latino visual arts. All these, we believe, are important vehicles for making the realities of race come alive for white people.

We try to ensure that most of the people involved in the formal and informal interactions organized by SDS are people of color. Sometimes we have to rearrange the makeup of meetings to get a broader range, including people who carry little formal power. Our funders, for example, now meet with the larger program staff, which is predominantly composed of people of color, and discussions with the district's evaluation staff now include evaluation liaisons, primarily people of color, from our school/community partnerships.

These efforts are slow and may even feel a bit cumbersome at first, but the effects are immediate and powerful, and the incentive to stick with them is strong indeed. Such efforts empower all of us. They free people of color to express the strength of their feelings and experiences. They invite white people to listen hard. They allow all of us to build schools that create the respect for racial and ethnic diversity on which our community depends.

Developmental Evaluation: An Approach for Empowerment-Oriented and Multicultural Programs
Michael Quinn Patton

Michael Quinn Patton is former president of the American Evaluation Association and the author of six major evaluation books, including Utilization-

Focused Evaluation. *He is a technical adviser to SDS and a trainer for evaluation processes as well as methods.*

My evaluation practice has been built on the premise that the values and methods of any particular evaluation should be matched to and appropriate for the program being evaluated. When a program is exploratory and developmental, therefore, the evaluation should be exploratory and developmental. Where the program aims to be empowering of participants, the evaluation should likewise be an empowering process.

Foundations are often willing to take the risk of trying things at the cutting edge, moving into uncharted territory, and working with grantees over time to develop genuinely new approaches to societal problems. In uncharted territory there are no maps. Indeed, in the early stages of exploration there may not even be any destination (goal) other than the exploration itself. One has to learn the territory to figure out what destination one wants to reach.

SDS, in my judgment, is an exemplar of a developmental grant. There is clearly a need to support diversity in schools; it is not at all clear how best to do that. SDS is exploring and developing a bottom-up, community-based approach. It invites local communities of color to play a substantive and meaningful role in the local schools. It asks parents and community people to work with educators to change school environments in support of diversity. For the process to work, for it to be genuinely empowering and bottom-up, the local community must struggle with setting its own ends and working to accomplish them. Under such conditions, it would be not only inappropriate but also potentially damaging for an external, foundation-funded evaluator to force premature articulation of clear, specific, measurable goals in accordance with traditional evaluation models.

Instead, the evaluator can become an enabling partner in the process, supporting the local community, program staff members, and school people in discovering what they want to accomplish and learning how to articulate claims about the differences they are committed to making. Some of these elements are similar to those found in formative evaluation, but there are important differences. Formative evaluation typically assumes that ultimate goals are known, and that the issue is how best to reach them. By contrast, developmental evaluation is preformative in the sense that it is *part of the process of developing* goals and implementation strategies. Developmental evaluation brings the logic and tools of evaluation into the early stages of community, organization, and program development.

In a developmental approach, the articulation of goals, claims, and supporting measures is one of the *outcomes* of the process, rather than one of the foreordained *determinants* of the process. Moreover, the goals, claims, and measures that develop during the process may change as the explorers of the new territory come to a better understanding of the lay of the land.

When clear, specific, measurable goals are established at the moment a grant is made, the struggle of community people to determine their own ends is summarily preempted, and they are once again disempowered—this time in the name of evaluation.

The logic of evaluation can be a powerful force for helping people clarify their thinking and become rigorous in holding themselves accountable. The highest form of accountability is self-accountability. If the community learns to hold itself accountable for its own aims, that is much more empowering than to be held accountable by external funders. This means that much of the evaluation activity in a developmental approach involves training local people to use evaluation logic and helping them develop their own goals, claims, criteria, and methods.

This kind of process clearly takes time. Much evaluation methodology assumes the accomplishment of concrete, measurable outcomes in one or two years, but community development processes take five to ten years. In our rapidly changing world, it would be absurd to force immediate commitment to the unknown goals and criteria of a five- to ten-year process. It is possible to make some commitments and specify some things (for example, active involvement of diverse groups of people, or ongoing articulation of developmental goals by participants in the process), but even these must be negotiated as part of the process.

I hasten to add that this process does not lack accountability. Rather, it is a developmental process that places primary accountability where it belongs—with the community and school people who have the most at stake. Of course, this takes trust and involves substantial risk, but that too is in the nature of development efforts conducted in uncharted territory. The potential benefits of doing things right are substantial. A developmental evaluation can capture those ultimate benefits over time in ways that are useful and understandable to participants, as well as to funders and the larger world.

Implementing the Developmental Evaluation Approach
Stacey Hueftle Stockdill

Stacey Hueftle Stockdill is president of EnSearch, Inc., of Minnesota. She earned her Ph.D., with a specialization in educational evaluation, from the University of Minnesota. She is the lead evaluator for SDS, with overall responsibility for coordinating the various levels and types of evaluation in the developmental process.

I feel that I am on new ground when, as a white female, I attempt to evaluate a multicultural education program. Fortunately, my training in intercultural communication helps to ground me in this new evaluation world. Nevertheless, much of my training in evaluation principles has had to be examined, redefined, and, in many cases, discarded.

I was trained to look at measures of central tendency, listen to the majority view, and recognize dispersion but, more frequently than not, discard the "isolates." In moving into evaluating SDS, the questions became "Who is the majority? What viewpoint should be identified as central when the distribution is rectangular or multimodal?"

My training taught me that carefully developed data-collection instruments could obtain the needed information validly and reliably. Now I am learning that my white female culture got in the way, and that I was isolated from critical pieces of information. For example, it was only through visits to Cambodian families' homes that the Cambodian staff member could determine their concerns about their children's education. It was only through telephone calls by African American parents to other African American parents that we learned of the racism experienced by their children. It was only because of the cultural sensitivity of Saint Paul American Indians in Unity that eighteen of twenty Indian parents attended a meeting and shared the depth of their frustration about the failure of schools to educate their children.

In SDS, I have been forced to break away from some basic evaluation assumptions: that numbers are important, that giving negative feedback is an important function, and that evaluation principles can be applied to any setting. I learned that not all cultures value counting exercises, that the style in which many Americans give negative feedback directly violates the norms of some cultures, and that evaluation is greatly affected by the extent to which program and administrative decision making is democratic and egalitarian rather than autocratic and hierarchical.

The original SDS evaluation design used a formative-summative approach that sought to determine definitions of goals that would be constant across all components of the program, collect qualitative information about program activities to use for formative purposes, and collect baseline data that would be used for summative purposes. Review of these design elements brought the realization that this traditional approach was both inappropriate and inadequate. It assumed that all the target populations had common strengths and needs, that the program would develop a single standardized model of intervention, that the model would become stabilized early in the life of the program, and that specific outcomes could be measured with an experimental design. None of those assumptions applied to the SDS program. There was incongruence between the activities of the program and those of the evaluation. The developmental approach proposed by Patton (1986) gave us a way of matching the evaluation process to the nature of the SDS program.

Developmental Evaluation Process

The first step in implementing the developmental evaluation approach was to help the SDS program staff, advisory committee, and partnership management teams make "claims" statements regarding the SDS program. Claims represented the participants' commitment to what would change as a result of SDS activities. We purposefully avoided a hierarchy of goals and objectives (although we do use the term *goal*) because of the formalistic and often negative connotations of that language. Using the notion of claims was intended as a straightforward way to get community and program participants to state what they were committed to changing—not hopes or funding priorities, but real expectations for and commitment to change.

Because SDS is built on principles of consensus in decision making and meaningful involvement of all stakeholders, the program staff, advisory committee, and partnership management teams worked together to define the claims for the SDS program. It was critical that the claims be developed and owned by those responsible for the program's activities and impacts throughout the community and schools, rather than by a small group of administrators and evaluators.

We found it important to help participants distinguish between program *claims*, subject to evaluation, and program *assumptions*, dependent on research findings. In the developmental design, the research premise was the theoretical assumption on which an overall SDS claim was based. Basic educational premises derive from research and therefore did not have to be proved by the program evaluation. This meant that our limited evaluation resources did not have to be used for investigation and verification of research-based premises but could be used instead for gathering information to support program development.

The SDS evaluation team is responsible for documenting the extent to which program claims are realized. For example, the SDS program is based in part on the educational research premise that relationships among teachers, students, and parents are critical to students' success and that those relationships are most supportive of students' development when they are based on mutual respect and cultural sensitivity. Neither the program nor the evaluation bears the burden of testing this research premise; instead, the evaluation focuses on describing and documenting the nature and effects of the relationships among SDS participants, without attempting to construct a design that would test more basic research premises, especially causal premises.

The claims document (see Exhibit 2.1) was distributed to the program staff, the partnership management teams, and the advisory committee for review and critique. Each school/community partnership reviewed the program claims and developed its own unique partnership claims. The partnerships had the options of embracing the SDS program claims as their own, accepting some of the claims as their own, and/or developing other claims. I worked with evaluation representatives from each of the partnerships to develop draft claims statements, to be redistributed to the partnership management teams for review and critique.

Exhibit 2.1. Sample SDS Claims Statement

Goal: School staff will increase their professional effectiveness in teaching students of color.

Research Premise: Relationships among teachers, students, and parents are critical to students' success, and those relationships are most supportive of students' development when they are based on mutual respect and cultural sensitivity.

Outcome Claims	*Potential Measures*
School Claims	
1. School staff interact with students, families, and communities with cultural awareness, warmth, and sensitivity—on the phone, in person, and in written communication. They use proper pronunciation of names, arrange children's seating to provide for integrated classroom environments, avoid racial jokes and innuendo, and confront prejudice when expressed by children or adults.	Observations of staff Parent surveys
2. Teachers conduct parent/teacher conferences in a manner that acknowledges the expertise of parents regarding their own children and culture.	Observations of staff Parent surveys
3. School staff of all racial and national backgrounds have rapport and mutually respectful relationships.	Survey of staff Site visits
4. School staff use community resources in addressing students' strengths and needs.	Review of materials Observations of staff
System Claims	
1. District job descriptions and systems of performance review include expectations of racial and cultural sensitivity for all staff.	Document review
2. The school district successfully recruits and hires staff of color for all levels of administrative, professional, support, and civil service positions.	District statistics

At monthly meetings, the multicultural team of evaluation liaisons receives training in evaluation methodologies and issues and reviews the evidence on partnership activities, outcomes, and claims. A recent training session used *Standards for Evaluations of Educational Programs, Projects, and Materials* to stimulate discussion regarding evaluator credibility, information scope and selection, defensible information sources, justified conclusions, and objective reporting.

Lessons Learned

Lessons learned from the first two years of program operation have been summarized and released as a work in progress. The specific findings will not be surprising to experienced program staff members or evaluators. What is important about these lessons is how they were developed, shared, discussed, and used by the SDS program staff and the school/community partnerships. Facilitating serious reflection on these kinds of lessons is one of the important ways in which evaluation is being used to support program development. A portion of the Lessons Learned report is presented as follows (Stockdill, 1991).

Lessons Learned Report
Establishing School/Community Partnerships:

Mutual commitment to problem solving was necessary for healthy partnership development. Any partnership that survived had or was able to develop a structure for raising issues, resolving problems, and reaching compromise. One essential element was commitment to improving success for children of color by solving problems with culturally sensitive methods. Successful partnerships were able to admit their problems and knew that there would be commitment to working through the relevant issues. In less successful partnerships, such commitment was sometimes lacking. In public, the less successful partnerships gave the appearance of being united. In private, their members described problems with conflict resolution, trust, and shared goals.

> They might not always agree, but people must cooperate with each other and respect each other. These factors promote partnership success [SDS staff member].

Issues and problems were more easily resolved when partnership members shared a vision. A shared vision could help sustain a partnership in difficult times; when team members recognized that they all had the same mission, it was easier for them to resolve issues and overcome difficulties.

> We learned not to lose track of the whole picture, and not to let the little setbacks and failures stop us [evaluation liaison].

> When we got a clear understanding of where we were all going, that is what really pulled us together [evaluation liaison].

> The goals were bigger than any individual person [evaluation liaison].

Stability in the makeup of the original partnership management teams contributed to success. When there were changes, success was reduced. Difficulties arose when members of the team who first developed a vision left the partnership.

> A lot of the players who wrote the proposal left. . . . [We got] a whole new group of people . . . with a totally different agenda and not with the same view or same purpose. . . . Getting everybody's goals together in the right direction was a difficult process [evaluation liaison].

> You start something with teachers [and principals], and they move out and around, so you don't get any groundwork with them before they move again [evaluation liaison].

> When you constantly change [people] like that, I don't see how there's going to be the job accomplished. [The new people] come with their own biases, their own ideas [evaluation liaison].

Final Reflections
Stacey Hueftle Stockdill, Rose Marie Duhon-Sells,
Ruth Anne Olson, Michael Quinn Patton

The developmental evaluation design for SDS is still emerging as the program changes in response to lessons learned. It is premature to judge the overall effectiveness of this evaluation approach. In this chapter, we have attempted to share some of what we have learned so far, with emphasis on why a developmental evaluation strategy is particularly appropriate for this kind of multicultural, community-based program.

We have certainly learned that everyone involved in the program needs to understand how developmental evaluation differs from traditional evaluation approaches. People must understand that the most important outcome is the insight gained from experience. This has been difficult for many because, in past experiences with evaluators, evaluation has been part of a win-lose game, and the evaluators generally won. In developmental evaluation, program staff members and school/community participants become partners with the evaluation team. The idea is to learn, and to make modifications on the basis of what is learned. With this approach and the active involvement of communities of color, all cultural perspectives are respected, the program can grow, and useful information can be obtained for further program development. Like the vision of SDS, the vision of developmental evaluation has been difficult to communicate. It takes time to build the mutual trust and respect that facilitate clear communication across diverse perspectives.

This chapter speaks with many voices. As such, it does not follow a traditional scholarly format. We began with the voices of SDS staff members—people of color who have powerfully articulated their problems with inappropriate evaluation designs and insensitive evaluators. We then presented our experiences with and perspectives on multicultural education and developmental evaluation. The reader has been asked to make sense of the different perspectives and piece process and content together from different points of view. This is not a traditionally cohesive chapter, and multicultural evaluation also is not traditionally cohesive. That is the challenge and the reward of this new direction for program evaluation.

References

Grant, C. "Multicultural Education: Examining the Why, What, and How." *Newsletter of the National Association for Multicultural Education,* 1991, *1* (1), 4–5.

Joint Committee on Standards for Educational Evaluation. *Standards for Evaluations of Educational Programs, Projects, and Materials.* New York: McGraw-Hill, 1981.

Patton, M. Q. *Utilization-Focused Evaluation.* (2nd ed.) Newbury Park, Calif.: Sage, 1986.

Sleeter, C., and Grant, C. "An Analysis of Multicultural Education in the United States." *Harvard Education Review,* 1988, *57,* 421–444.

Stockdill, S. H. *Lessons Learned Evaluation Report.* (Report prepared for the SDS Donor Review Board.) St. Paul, Minn.: Saint Paul Foundation, 1991.

STACEY HUEFTLE STOCKDILL is president of EnSearch, Inc., of Minnesota.

ROSE MARIE DUHON-SELLS is cofounder and executive chair of the National Association for Multicultural Education. She is also dean of the College of Education of Southern University, Baton Rouge, Louisiana.

RUTH ANNE OLSON has had a private consulting practice in educational program design and evaluation since 1971.

MICHAEL QUINN PATTON is former president of the American Evaluation Association and the author of six major books on evaluation.

*Advocates of the participation of multiple stakeholders in
evaluation seldom include minority participants in the process,
yet ethnic and racial minorities have the most at stake in the
evaluation of social services and educational programs.*

Primary Inclusion of Culturally Diverse Minority Program Participants in the Evaluation Process

Anna-Marie Madison

Evaluation theorists and methodologists have presented various models for inclusion of clients in the evaluation process. Such models as the discrepancy evaluation model (Steinmetz, 1989), the responsive evaluation model (Stake, 1989), and the utilization-focused evaluation model (Patton, 1986) emphasize the role of client participation in program evaluation. The client perspective, however, is defined in terms of the role of managers and program staff as major stakeholders in the evaluation process. Although other stakeholders are acknowledged as important, program managers and staff are described as the dominant stakeholders.

Racial and ethnic minorities and the poor, who are disproportionately represented among social program participants, have been omitted as stakeholder participants in evaluation. As Lincoln (1991) points out, most people who evaluate social programs know very little about the minority program participants' world view, the appropriateness of program interventions in meeting their needs, or the programs' personal consequences for these clients.

Evaluators who have had little contact with minority low-income groups may not be the best persons to determine the appropriateness of various program strategies in addressing the needs of minorities or the efficacy of social programs in achieving desired outcomes. In many cases, middle-class program managers and administrative decision makers, including many middle-class minorities, are too removed from the world views and experiences of the program participants to enhance evaluators' understanding of the program participants. Therefore, it is important that evaluators provide procedures for minority program participants to help them understand their world.

This chapter addresses the relevance of primary input from the minority program participants in defining evaluation and interpreting program outcomes. *Primary inclusion* refers to direct participation of program participants in all phases of program development, from the conceptualization of problems to the evaluation and the interpretation of findings.

Conceptualization of Social Problems

The first role, perhaps one of the most important roles that minority program participants can play in program planning and design, entails minorities' input into the conceptual definition of problems. Conceptual constructs of reality are derived from individual interpretations of the world (Edwards, 1987; House, 1983). Kimmel (1988) argues that values influence perceptions of potentially damaging social conditions, as well as the selection of social interventions to ameliorate identified problems.

Social program planners and evaluators must acknowledge that how they perceive the program participants and their problems is derived from personal values and assumptions about the group. To relate social conditions to the real world of the targeted population, the evaluator first has to see the problems from the perspective of that population. If social programs are to make sense to minority participants, the conceptual constructs for defining social problems must encompass the cultural context of the participants.

The importance of culture in the definition of social problems and in the design of social programs is widely discussed in the cross-cultural research (Smith, 1991; Cuthbert, 1985; Patton, 1986). Many of the issues discussed from an international cross-cultural perspective are also relevant to an understanding of the dynamics of cultural diversity in the United States.

The dynamics of dominant colonial culture–third-world culture interactions can be used to describe patterns of cultural dominance and subordination in this country. For example, minority low-income ethnic communities are very much like third-world countries in that they are politically and economically dependent on the dominant groups in society for survival, yet they maintain their own core social values that guide their understanding of their living environment and their responses to the environment. Therefore, understanding the cultural context of the community (Smith, 1991) is an important dimension in understanding the social reality of low-income minority communities. Failure to take cultural dimensions into consideration can lead to misinterpretations of social reality.

The importance of the cultural context in problem definition is emphasized by House (1983). He contends that reality is defined in terms of the metaphors used to structure images of the real world. The appropriateness of the metaphors selected to describe the real world is based on cultural interpretations of the world. Therefore, according to House, social reality is derived from the culturally guided selecting, naming, and relating of elements within a chosen framework (House, 1983). To illustrate this point, House presents two views of the slums, each derived from an individual cultural interpretation. Whereas one individual may view slums as "natural communities," another may view them as "communities in decay." This example illustrates that how the "problem" is conceptualized is critical to the "solution" that emerges. The policy solution to the problem of slums will differ according to how the phenomenon is viewed.

Smith's framework (1991) for understanding the cultural context of evaluations, and the logic of House's argument (1983) concerning the construction of social reality, provide support for the notion that the cultural setting of minority communities is important to an understanding of social realities in those communities. Definitions of social problems must emerge from constructions of reality within the cultural contexts and experiences of the individuals affected by solutions. If the cultural context is not incorporated into our understanding of the environments where we define problems and conduct evaluations, then evaluation may be limited in its ability to inform.

Several available methodologies allow residents of minority communities to participate in the problem-definition stage of program planning. The responsive evaluation model (Stake, 1989) provides a procedure for negotiation of an appropriate construct of reality, which would encompass both the world view of minority program participants and the dominant world view. Shared construction is a deliberate process that allows various stakeholders in evaluation to reconcile their differences and reach consensus on definitions of reality. The constructivist paradigm (Guba and Lincoln, 1989) also provides an interactive process for understanding the environment from which the intended beneficiaries construct their views of reality. The developmental, community-based approach (see Chapter Two) illustrates a method for primary inclusion of the minority community in all phases of the program.

One aspect of the primary inclusion approach that may be problematic is the time it takes to implement the process. Given the vast amount of time this approach requires, it may represent a challenge to evaluators who work under stringent time constraints. Another potentially troublesome aspect is that the inclusion of minority program participants in the conceptualization of social problems may intimidate professional evaluators and managers who are not accustomed to sharing power with individuals different from themselves. The positive aspect of this approach is that the benefits of incorporating the targeted population's world view into the conceptual definition of the problem may increase the chances of the program's success in meeting the participants' needs.

Problems Inherent in the Utilization of
Existing Social Theory

Advocates of theory-driven evaluation suggest that social science theory should be used to assist planners and evaluators in designing program theory (Bickman, 1987, 1990; Chen and Rossi, 1983, 1980; Chen, 1990; Smith, 1990). These evaluators advocate the use of social science theory in establishing program strategies and measuring outcomes. Although the concept of theory-driven evaluation has merit, there are some dangers inherent in its application when the cultural context of the theories is not taken into consideration.

Construction of social theory is based on experience and agreement about reality, in terms of how we interpret the real world and what we agree is real. Thus, both experiential reality and consensual reality are derived from one's culture. Social science theory regarding social problems in the United States is based on a dominant cultural interpretation of the real world. The concern is whether current social theories, derived from a unidimensional cultural orientation, are adequate for constructing program theory to address problems derived from multicultural settings.

Although social scientists have labored for years to free themselves of cultural bias, some have conceded that there is no such thing as culture-free research (House, 1990; Hage, 1972; Kaplan, 1964). Inherent in all research are biases. In evaluation research, House (1990) observes, these biases are often implicit, rather than explicit: "Many values . . . remain . . . , hidden in ways not discernible, even to ourselves, and while these embedded values may not be harmful or wrong, sometimes they are both" (p. 23). House says that, in many cases, personal biases are translated into methods of discovery and validation of truth. To illustrate the impact of investigators' biases on validation of truth, House presents both extreme and less extreme examples. Other examples of investigator error (and the consequences of repetitions of errors in research) are illuminated by Hilliard (1989).

The cultural biases inherent in how middle-class white researchers interpret the experiences of low-income minorities may lead to erroneous assumptions and faulty propositions concerning causal relationships, to invalid social theory, and consequently to invalid program theory. Descriptive theories derived from faulty premises, which have been legitimized in the literature as existing knowledge, may have negative consequences for program participants. Moreover, such errors may have immediate effects on the lives of the minorities who are the potential beneficiaries of social policies (House, 1990).

Opportunities for cultural bias in theory construction can be traced to the conceptual stage. In the context of scientific inquiry, concepts are symbols of the real world, which are used to transmit perceptions and information (House, 1983; Nachmias and Nachmias, 1981). As Kaplan (1964) observes, scientific concepts have meaning only because scientists mean something by them. The meaning assigned to an abstraction emerges from cultural interpretation of one's experience. The selection of one set of descriptors over another in assigning literal meaning to a concept is not culture-free in that the criterion itself is not culture-free. Since there is an indefinite number of dimensions, criteria must be established to determine which ones to select.

The conceptual problem is even more pronounced when nonvariable concepts are used to describe social conditions. The major problem, as Hage (1972) illustrates, is that descriptive tags lack agreement on what is meant. This lack of clarity makes it difficult to order relationships. Examples of nonvariable concepts are *hardcore unemployable, underprivileged, underclass, culturally deprived, economically disadvantaged, at-risk population,* and *chronically unemployed.* Besides the problem in providing a conceptual definition of nonvariable concepts, negative social prejudices underlie each of these conceptual descriptors. One certainly could not interpret such tags as value-free or culturally neutral.

Once an error has been introduced into the initial conceptual framework, it is carried over into the ordering of relationships between concepts. Assumptions about causal conditions are not exempt from partiality. Hage (1972) stresses that the selection of propositions and assumptions and the ordering of links within theoretical constructs are derived from the individual, with all his or her prejudices. Errors introduced at this level can be extremely damaging when cultural and socioeconomic biases underlie the systematic ordering of variables to explain causal relationships. Program models based on theory derived from defective causal explanations may contribute little of value to changing conditions for program participants.

Another potentially troublesome aspect of social science theory is that distinctions between assertions and affirmations are often not made. What is presented as theory may be a complex set of assumptions, propositions, and hypotheses that have never been affirmed. For example, the "culture of poverty" theory of life in the inner city was used as the rationale for many social action programs during the 1960s. In reality, what was referred to by many social scientists as the "culture of poverty" theory was no more than a hypothesis. This hypothesis had never been affirmed, yet many social scientists accepted the "culture of poverty" theory as an explanation of the real world, and many valuable dollars that could have been used to eradicate poverty were wasted on feeble programs designed to provide ethnic minorities with cultural alternatives.

Therefore, before we begin to use existing theory to construct causal program models, it is critical that we consider the cultural validity of the theoretical construct from which a particular theory is derived. As Przeworski and Teune (1970) point out, identification of the social system in which a given phenomenon occurs is part of the explanation. One must be able to determine which factors are specific to the culture of a community and which cut across all communities.

Even with intersubjectivity as a control to detect personal biases in social science research, when the majority of the researchers share common cultural biases and myths concerning groups different from themselves, similarities in values may cancel researchers' ability to check one another. Theorists draw on a common experience and a common intellectual framework as part of their enculturation (House, 1983). To overcome some of the limitations in existing theory, perhaps evaluators will need to generate their own knowledge base and develop causal models useful in program development.

The integrative approach to program theory development (Chen, 1990) incorporates both stakeholders' viewpoints and social science knowledge. This approach provides an opportunity for the evaluator to include not only the manager but also the intended program beneficiaries in the knowledge-generating process. The integrative approach provides opportunities to incorporate the cultural context into explanations of social reality. At a minimum, it provides a mechanism by which checkpoints can be established for reconciling disparities in cultural interpretations of the real world.

There are several rationales for the inclusion of minorities in this process. First, input from the intended beneficiaries of programs may enlighten evaluators and program developers about social realities as they are experienced. Second, the program beneficiaries are in a better position than anyone else to explain what has worked and what has not worked for them in the past, allowing for better understanding of cause-effect relationships between program interventions and outcomes. Such information could lead to more efficient use of resources. Third, program participants may provide an opportunity for observation of positive models, rather than the deficit models usually used in the construction of social theories about minorities.

Social Program Evaluation and Interpretation of Evaluation Findings

Initial bias associated with individual decisions about appropriate evaluation methods is related to beliefs about the relative value of alternative ways of knowing (Guba and Lincoln, 1989; Cronbach, 1982; Kimmel, 1988). Discussing methodological conflicts among social scientists, Kaplan (1964) observes that the more we learn how to do something, the harder it is to learn to do it differently. Resistance to the expansion of evaluation methodology is rooted in conformity, which in itself limits the application of alternative ways of knowing.

Kaplan (1964) cautions that too much emphasis on the perfection of methods can obstruct doing the job at all. Perhaps evaluators should heed Kaplan's advice that "it is less important to draw a fine line between what is 'scientific' and what is not than to cherish every opportunity for scientific growth" (p. 28).

Ideological and epistemological disputes should not overshadow the importance of seeking the truth for the betterment of society. As a social practice, evaluation entails a public responsibility (House, 1990). This public responsibility should include ascertaining the truth about programs. Evaluators have a responsibility to those most affected by the program under review to use every method available for seeking the truth. The ultimate goal of evaluators should be to ascertain the closest approximation of truth about the impact of social policy on the real world of program participants.

The selection of evaluation methods should take account of the culture-specific factors that may be encountered in the implementation of various research designs. Cultural factors should also be considered in the selection of data-collection methods and in data verification. Cuthbert (1985) notes that if the targeted population's cooperation is to be expected, its values, beliefs, and traditions should be taken into consideration in the evaluation design. Faase and Pujdak (1987) argue that evaluators who share the basic values of the targeted population more easily see these issues in a cultural context and more clearly address them.

The evaluator should also realize that views about reality and about the nature of change can lead to different assumptions about appropriate evaluation modes (Cuthbert, 1985). Conflicting ideologies concerning what is real may inhibit clear understanding of the evaluator's information. To obtain comprehensive understanding of a program's impact on those who are its objects, participation by the targeted groups in the evaluation is necessary.

If social justice is a goal of redistributive policy, then evaluation should address issues of social justice in the assessment of a program's impact. In the selection of evaluation methods, the evaluator should consider the ability of the evaluation design to answer questions about social justice in terms of the value of the program in the context of the program participants' expectations and social realities. To address issues of social justice, a broad range of approaches to evaluation is necessary. Primary inclusion of program participants in the selection of appropriate evaluation strategies can provide cultural credibility to the interpretation and application of evaluation findings. Program participants can also offer insight into whether moral questions of social justice have been addressed in the evaluation design.

Conclusion

This chapter has raised issues concerning the active participation of program participants in the evaluation of social programs. It has offered suggestions for including program participants in the continuum of activities, from defining social conditions and problems to evaluating the impact of social programs on social problems. Acknowledging that evaluation is by nature subjective, the question that I pose here to the evaluation community is this: Why not make the subjectivity of evaluation more democratic, more inclusive, and, as Lincoln (1991) suggests, a tool for empowering program participants as advocates in their own best interest?

References

Bickman, L. (ed.). *Using Program Theory in Evaluation.* New Directions for Program Evaluation, no. 3. San Francisco: Jossey-Bass, 1987.

Bickman, L. (ed.). *Advances in Program Theory.* New Directions for Program Evaluation, no. 47. San Francisco: Jossey-Bass, 1990.

Chen, H. T. "Issues in Constructing Program Theory." In L. Bickman (ed.), *Advances in Program Theory.* New Directions for Program Evaluation, no. 47. San Francisco: Jossey-Bass, 1990.

Chen, H. T., and Rossi, P. H. "The Multi-Goal, Theory-Driven Approach to Evaluation: A Model Linking Basic and Applied Social Science." *Social Forces,* 1980, 59, 106-122.

Chen, H. T., and Rossi, P. H. "Evaluating with Sense: The Theory-Driven Approach." *Evaluation Review,* 1983, 7, 283-302.

Cronbach, L. J. *Designing Evaluations of Educational and Social Programs.* San Francisco: Jossey-Bass, 1982.

Cuthbert, M. "Evaluation Encounters in Third-World Settings: A Caribbean Perspective." In M. Patton (ed.), *Culture and Evaluation.* New Directions for Program Evaluation, no. 25. San Francisco: Jossey-Bass, 1985.

Edwards, P. K. "Conceptual and Methodological Issues in Evaluating Emergent Proposals." *Evaluation and Program Planning,* 1987, 10, 27-33.

Faase, T. P., and Pujdak, S. "Shared Understanding of Organizational Culture." In J. Nowakowski (ed.), *The Client Perspective on Evaluation.* New Directions for Program Evaluation, no. 36. San Francisco: Jossey-Bass, 1987.

Guba, E. G., and Lincoln, Y. S. *Fourth-Generation Evaluation.* Newbury Park, Calif.: Sage, 1989.

Hage, J. *Techniques and Problems of Theory Construction in Sociology.* New York: Wiley, 1972.

Hilliard, A. G., III. "Kemetic (Egyptian) Historical Revision: Implications for Cross-Cultural Evaluation and Research in Education." *Evaluation Practice,* 1989, 10, 7-21.

House, E. R. "How We Think About Evaluation." In E. R. House (ed.), *Philosophy of Evaluation.* New Directions for Program Evaluation, no. 19. San Francisco: Jossey-Bass, 1983.

House, E. R. "Methodology and Justice." In K. A. Sirotnik (ed.), *Evaluation and Social Justice: Issues in Public Education.* New Directions for Program Evaluation, no. 45. San Francisco: Jossey-Bass, 1990.

Kaplan, A. *The Conduct of Inquiry: Methodology for Behavioral Science.* Scranton, Pa.: Chandler, 1964.

Kimmel, A. J. *Ethics and Values in Applied Research.* Newbury Park, Calif.: Sage, 1988.

Lincoln, Y. S. "The Arts and Sciences of Program Evaluation." *Evaluation Practice,* 1991, 12, 1-7.

Nachmias, D., and Nachmias, C. *Research Methods in the Social Sciences.* New York: St. Martin's Press, 1981.

Patton, M. Q. *Utilization-Focused Evaluation.* Newbury Park, Calif.: Sage, 1986.

Przeworski, A., and Teune, H. *The Logic of Comparative Inquiry.* New York: Wiley, 1970.

Smith, N. L. "Using Path Analysis to Develop and Evaluate Program Theory and Impact." In L. Bickman (ed.), *Advances in Program Theory*. New Directions for Program Evaluation, no. 47. San Francisco: Jossey-Bass, 1990.

Smith, N. L. "Evaluation Reflections: The Context of Investigations in Cross-Culture Evaluations." *Studies in Educational Evaluation*, 1991, *17*, 3-21.

Stake, R. E. "Program Evaluation, Particularly Responsive Evaluation." In G. F. Madaus, M. Scriven, and D. L. Stufflebeam (eds.), *Evaluation Models: Viewpoints on Educational and Human Services Evaluation*. Boston: Kluwer-Nijhoff, 1989.

Steinmetz, A. "The Discrepancy Evaluation Model." In G. F. Madaus, M. Scriven, and D. L. Stufflebeam (eds.), *Evaluation Models: Viewpoints on Educational and Human Services Evaluation*. Boston: Kluwer-Nijhoff, 1989.

ANNA-MARIE MADISON is associate professor of public administration at the University of North Texas, Denton.

Using standardized test scores to determine program effectiveness may contribute to further inequities.

Standardized Tests and Program Evaluation: Inappropriate Measures in Critical Times

Ceasar L. McDowell

> Nobody scores 100 on the test except the guy who made it. Made it. Made it. And nobody can be like him. Only him. Like him. Because he made it. Test scores prove the point. Only so much room at the top. What good would a test be that doesn't prove what anybody with good sense knows already to be true? A bell curve. Rings true. For whom? Is it tolling?
> —John Edgar Wideman, 1990, p. 172

Over the last several years, various sectors of the United States have been engaged in an ongoing debate regarding the potential impact of the changing demographic profile of the country. While most of this concern for the "browning of America" is based on the possible impact on the economic viability of the country, schools and schooling have been the focus of the debate. A plethora of reports link work-force productivity to the inadequate educational preparation of high school students and young adults. Schools, universities, and other educational agencies, spurred by these reports, are engaged in the development and implementation of programs that will eradicate the at-risk status of the nation by focusing on improvement of services and educational outcomes for the population of students most at risk.

Not surprisingly, most of these at-risk students come from those groups (African American, Latino, Asian, Native American, and poor) that are often ill served by education yet are simultaneously becoming the majority of students educated by the public school system. As of four years ago, over 50 percent of the students in the twenty-five largest school districts in the United States were students of color ("Using Demographic Data . . . ," 1988).

A key instrument in efforts to identify and certify effective programs has been standardized test scores. On the basis of results from varied types of standardized tests—ranging from the Scholastic Aptitude Test (SAT) to the National Teachers Exam (NTE) and achievement tests developed by local educational agencies—the effectiveness of programs, schools, and teachers is evaluated. In New Jersey, for example, standardized test scores are used to determine whether schools are in compliance with the minimum standards of the state.

The increase in standardized testing is partly the result of declining governmental resources. As federal, state, and local revenues decline, there is increased political pressure for publicly funded programs to provide clear proof of their effectiveness, in the form of measurable outcomes. Coupled with this demand is the desire among many business, political, and educational leaders for the establishment of national educational standards and a common means of measuring the achievement of such standards.

On the surface, the push to use standardized instruments in program evaluation appears appropriate for assessing programs' effectiveness. Nevertheless, two facts suggest that increased emphasis on standardized tests in evaluation may result in an understating of the effectiveness of programs that serve a substantial number of minority students.

First, differential performance by black and white test-takers has been found to be fairly substantial in studies of both educational and employment tests in the United States. American Indians, some Asian Americans, black Americans, Native Pacific Islanders, and other minority groups tend to score significantly lower than their white counterparts on many tests (National Commission on Testing and Public Policy, 1990).

Second, the performance differences of racial, cultural, and linguistic minority groups and women on standardized tests is attributable to factors that are not necessarily ameliorable by educational programs. Among these are the existence of real inequities of opportunity (such as lower average income and higher unemployment rates), technical limitations of standardized measures, and the cultural orientation of tests (toward the topics, language, and ways of knowing of one group, as opposed to those of others). While it is not clear how these three factors are interrelated, it is clear that, individually and collectively, they limit the possibility and practicality of constructing standardized testing instruments that do not evoke unfair differential performance. Accordingly, the use of standardized instruments in evaluation may inadvertently result in inaccurate assessment of the effectiveness of programs that serve large numbers of minority students.

In testing policy and practice, much of the attention to culture's influence on test performance is focused on how the language and socialization values of one group differ (deviate) from those of a narrowly described "norm." As a consequence, efforts to address cultural differences in testing mostly concentrate on acculturating the individual from the low-performing group to the ascribed normative pattern of the higher-performing group. Reconceptualizing the methods of measurement and reexamining the methods for interpreting responses are rarely at the center of efforts to make testing culturally appropriate. In this instance, the test becomes the end, rather than the means to an end—providing appropriate tools for measuring acquired knowledge. Nevertheless, it is culture's relationship to cognition, language, and social capital that accounts for its impact on testing.

In this chapter, the discussion of culture and cultural biases attempts to remove the normative (and therefore deficit) emphasis on differences that is often the basis of discussions about culture and testing. Accordingly, *culture* is defined here as the commonly held *experiences* of a particular group of people that inform and shape the social and privately held values, forms of expression, and ways of knowing that bond the members of that group. Drawing on Omi and Winant's notion (1986) of the relationship of race, class, and gender to the prominent spheres of social conflict in this country, and drawing on Ogbu's concept (1979, 1981, 1985, 1986) of fictive kinship, this definition of culture subsumes race, class, and gender. (While I do refer to particular racial groups or to women in cultural terms, I do not necessarily argue that there is a unifying black, women's, or working-class culture.)

This chapter seeks to provide evaluators with an overview of the various ways in which culture influences test performance, inevitably rendering the use of standardized tests for program evaluation suspect in a culturally diverse society. The first part of the chapter explores the relationship between culture and cognition. The second part examines language effects on test performance. The third part explores the social and political consequences of culture for test performance.

Culture and Cognition

Culture mediates the cognitive functions and/or repertoires of people (Ogbu, 1985, 1986; Miller-Jones, 1989, in press; Vygotsky, 1978; Bronfenbrenner, 1979, 1982, 1986). To state that culture mediates cognition is not to say that culture prevents certain groups of people from learning or understanding particular ways of thinking or knowing, or that culture exclusively enables other groups in those realms. It is to say that culture helps determine how we first know yet does not limit our capacity to know or learn in other ways (Cole and Bruner, 1971). Accordingly, since cognition develops out of the social and historical evolution of the mind, cognition can be understood only as variant (Bronfenbrenner, 1989; Vygotsky, 1929, 1978).

One consequence of the variability of mental processes is that culture can mediate the cognitive formation of the mental models that individuals construct to represent the functioning of the world. By *mental model,* I mean the images we create in our minds to help us make meaning of the ideas, concepts, processes, and phenomena that emerge from the world around us. The mental models we hold affect our understanding of the world. Moreover, the use, construction, and importance of images differ from culture to culture. The image making of people can differ to the extent that people cannot understand the means by which experience becomes transformed into expression in an alien culture (Highwater, 1981), not to mention the messages themselves. Consequently, when we have to make meaning of or learn in a cultural context that is different from our own, our mental models can *"pervade, enable, and sometimes even disable"* our understanding and thinking (Perkins, 1986; emphasis in original).

The cumulative result of the variability in how people of different cultures construct their cognitive maps is that "the reasoning strategies associated with a task are not always obvious or given" (O'Connor, 1989, p. 157). Accordingly, our ability to map exact meaning from responses to standardized tasks is limited, at best.

Culture and Language

The fundamental explanation for the variation in test scores among students with limited English proficiency is that native speakers of a language differ from non-native speakers. The basic assertion is that the complexity of language renders impractical a process that is essential to the construction of a standardized test: the mapping of universal meanings to particular language constructs (see Labov, 1968, 1972; Williams, 1970). For example, black English vernacular (BEV) provides for greater variability in distinguishing habitual and momentary events. To cite an example offered by the linguist John Baugh, the sentence "The train is traveling at sixty miles per hour" could be expressed in two different ways in BEV, each denoting a difference in the type of movement the train is engaged in. "The train('s) traveling at sixty miles per hour" refers to the momentary status of a sixty-mile-per-hour train that may make frequent stops. "The train be traveling at sixty miles per hour" indicates a train that is traveling at an exact speed; this form usually would not be used to describe a train that makes frequent stops (Baugh, 1989, p. 402).

Within a given language, dialectical and vernacular differences limit the ability to infer meaning from responses to highly structured language-based assessments. Correspondingly, we can expect the same limited utility of language-based assessments for students with limited English proficiency, whether the assessment is written or oral (Bartel, Grill, and Bryden, 1973). There is agreement among many researchers, however, that language proficiency may be the most important factor in test performance for most test takers (William, 1983; Padilla, 1979; O'Connor, 1989; Valdez and Figueroa, in press). This assertion is particularly important, given the diversity of primary languages spoken in the United States.

It is estimated that there are 3.5 million linguistic-minority children of school age who have limited English proficiency (Olmedo, 1981). It is also estimated that in the United States today about two-thirds of the Asian American population speak languages other than English at home, and that about 20 percent of those five or older in this group may have limited English proficiency. Moreover, about 59 percent of Asian Americans are foreign-born immigrants (Tsang, 1989). A similar pattern is found among Hispanic students and members of other non–English-speaking immigrant and migrant groups, in which there is a vast amount of dialectical difference, as well as many levels of proficiency, in both English and the native language.

The impact of the figures regarding Asian Americans is evident in the performance profile of Asian Americans on tests like the SAT. While it is common to hear about the high SAT math scores of Asian Americans, the mean SAT verbal score for Asian Americans (395) is substantially lower than the 473 mean score of whites. Even among Asian American students whose best language is English, the same profile exists (SAT-V 427 versus 473). Among Asian Americans, moreover, there is evidence that this pattern may not dissipate with time. Asian American students who have been living in the United States for five years or less show little progress in verbal skills year to year, by comparison with other Asian Americans or whites (Tsang and Wing, 1985).

Culture as Capital

The "cultural capital" interpretation of performance differences on standardized tests suggests that, in the political economy of a nation, culture functions as capital (Aronowitz and Giroux, 1985; Bowles and Gintis, 1986). Accordingly, like other forms of capital, culture controls and mediates the social and political terrain of a society. It is a metric on which the value of individuals or groups of individuals is determined. D'Andrade's study (1973) of Hausa children of West Africa illustrates this point. According to D'Andrade, "It seems most probable that it is not a deficit in intelligence which makes for [their] poor performance [on a particular test], but instead a lack of experience in our special methods by which reality can be symbolized" (p. 19).

Much of the social difference in approaches to the demonstration of cognitive faculties is related to different competencies that are stressed in child-rearing practices. These differences in approach account for much of the failure of minority children in schools because some students come to school with "different rules of behavior for achievement and related competencies" (Ogbu, 1981, p. 414). Children have these different rules of behavior not because their parents are incapable of or lack "white middle-class capability in child rearing but because such is the requirement for their [the children's] competence in adult cultural/subsistence task[s]" in the environments where they must survive (Ogbu, 1981, p. 415).

Contemporary testing practices assume two culturally held values: first, that achievement is an individual accomplishment and, second, that such accomplishment should be publicly displayed. Most middle-class children have been socialized to accept these two values. Many non–middle-class children, as well as children from other cultures, do not share these values (see Gay and Abrahams, 1973; Briggs, 1984). As a result, many children have no clear idea of what testing is when they encounter it for the first time in school, nor have they grown up in environments where children are asked to give information to adults. For example, many American Indian cultures socialize children through nonverbal communication, emphasizing visual/spatial memory, visual/motor skills, and sequential visual memory over verbal skills. Many of these cultures also emphasize sharing and working together. The tests that these children encounter in school focus on verbal skills and force children to work alone. Because of the patterns of teaching in Navajo society, many Navajo children encountering a test for the first time see it literally as a game, not as an evaluation tool; the Navajo's first-grade middle-class Anglo peer perceives the test as a serious evaluation tool (McShane, 1989).

Tests and the Allocation of Opportunity

In May 1990, the National Commission on Testing and Public Policy (1990) released the results of its three-year study of the role of standardized testing in the educational, economic, and political life of the nation. The report describes the failure of current testing policies and practices to meet the educational and economic challenges facing American society. The commission found that testing "is overrelied upon, lacks adequate public accountability, sometimes leads to unfairness in the allocation of opportunities, and too often undermines vital social policies" (p. ix). Accordingly, the report articulates a vision for the future of testing that moves the enterprise away from identification and selection, toward development and enhancement of individual talent and toward promotion of productive, accountable, just institutions. These findings and recommendations were driven by the recognition that current dissatisfactions with the quality of the nation's schools, as well as the inability of businesses and the work force to compete effectively in an increasingly international marketplace, point to a crisis in human resources in the United States, a crisis characterized by an inability to nurture and make effective use of intellectual resources.

One key mechanism in the identification of human abilities and talents and the allocation of economic resources is and will continue to be standardized tests. Often referred to as *high-stakes testing,* the practice of relying on a single score from one standardized test to allocate opportunity is on the rise. For example, several states are now requiring their college sophomores to pass a standardized test in order to go on to the junior year. Grades are considered, but students who fail the so-called rising junior test cannot move on, even if they have straight A's. The cutoff scores used by these and other high-stakes tests are ultimately arbitrary. When the standard problems of measurement error are combined with the cultural limitations of standardized tests, the use of single "cut" scores often results in practices that allocate opportunity on the basis of race and gender rather than ability (National Commission on Testing and Public Policy, 1990; Hartigan and Wigdor, 1989).

An examination of the scoring differences among blacks and whites on tests that are used to allocate opportunity illustrates the extent to which arbitrary use of scores can and does limit opportunities for racial and cultural minority groups. In 1988, SAT scores of blacks, Puerto Ricans, Mexican Americans, and Asian Americans were lower than those of whites. For blacks, there was a 92-point difference; for Asian Americans, the difference was 37 points. Over the past several years, blacks have scored an average of 100 points below whites on the SAT. On the Graduate Record Exam, whites outscored all other racial groups that took the exam in 1988. Among students taking Florida's rising-junior test (the College-Level Academic Skills Test, or CLAST) for the first time, only 64 percent and 72 percent of blacks and Hispanics, respectively, passed the exam, compared with 92 percent of whites (National Commission on Testing and Public Policy, 1990).

Despite these differences, and despite our understanding that they are due to the limitations of standardized tests (not to the inability of minority students), there is growing pressure to increase the use of tests in the allocation of opportunity. Every day, educators and employers use test scores to decide which individuals will and will not have access to opportunities that could enhance their ability to pursue productive and enriching lives. Hardworking, intelligent students are denied access to educational programs in which they could have succeeded. Productive, capable workers are turned down for jobs that they could have performed effectively if given the chance. Five-year-old children are judged not ready for school programs expressly designed to get them ready for the academic and social demands of schooling. Men, women, and children of varied ethnic, linguistic, and cultural backgrounds are erroneously told that they lack the capacity to pursue their chosen careers and academic interests. This practice is clearly damaging to the lives and aspirations of the people who are excluded.

Conclusion

The significant changes in the U.S. population demonstrate that our ability to meet the needs of all people in this country will require the development of educational programs and procedures that can respond to the cultural breadth of all Americans. For evaluation to help build programs that will assist those who are least served by the schools, evaluators will have to be cautious in their use of instruments and methods that unfairly exploit the differences among people. High on the list of such instruments are standardized tests.

Culture plays an important role in test performance and in the possibility of creating truly standardized measures. Culture has this effect because it both informs the mental models that individuals construct to make meaning of the world and mediates the ways in which people demonstrate the knowledge they have. In Chapter Five of this volume, Davis articulates the complexity of considering one aspect of culture—race—as a variable in evaluation. His concern is the practice of using traditional comparative analytical frameworks to identify racial differences; mine is the inappropriate use of standardized test scores. Regardless of the frame used in evaluation, reliance on standardized testing instruments to assess programs' effectiveness can lead to miscalculation of effectiveness among programs that serve a large number of minority students. Several factors in test construction contribute to this problem, and culture is perhaps the least understood of these. As we move into the twenty-first century, however, culture and its antecedents, language and race, will become prominent themes in our efforts to design, implement, and evaluate effective educational programs. Accordingly, evaluators have a *need* and a *responsibility* to understand the role that culture plays in evaluation if they are to practice their craft responsibly and ethically.

References

Aronowitz, S., and Giroux, H. A. *Education Under Siege: The Conservative, Liberal, and Radical Debate Over Schooling.* Massachusetts: Bergin and Garvey, 1985.

Bartel, N. R., Grill, J. J., and Bryden, D. N. "Language Characteristics of Black Children: Implications for Assessment." *Journal of School Psychology,* 1973, *11* (4), 351–363.

Baugh, J. Untitled book review of E. Orr, *Twice as Less. Harvard Educational Review,* 1989, 58 (3), 402.

Bowles, S., and Gintis, H. *Democracy and Capitalism: Property, Community, and the Contradictions of Modern Social Thought.* New York: Basic Books, 1986.

Briggs, C. L. "Learning How to Ask: Native Metacommunicative Competence and the Incompetence of Fieldworkers." *Language and Society,* 1984, *13,* 1–28.

Bronfenbrenner, U. *The Ecology of Human Development.* Cambridge, Mass.: Harvard University Press, 1979.

Bronfenbrenner, U. "Child Development: The Hidden Revolution." In *National Research Council: Issues and Studies.* Washington, D.C.: National Academy Press, 1982.

Bronfenbrenner, U. "Ecology of the Family as a Context for Human Development." *Developmental Psychology*, 1986, *22*, 723-742.

Bronfenbrenner, U. "Ecological Systems Theory." In R. Vast (ed.), *Annals of Child Development*. Vol. 6. Greenwood, Conn.: JAI Press, 1989.

Cole, M., and Bruner, J. "Cultural Differences and Inferences of Intelligence." *American Psychologist*, 1971, *71*, 828-876.

D'Andrade, R. "Cultural Constructions of Reality." In L. Nader and T. W. Meretzki (eds.), *Cultural Illness and Health: Essays in Human Adaptation*. Washington, D.C.: American Anthropological Society, 1973.

Gay, G., and Abrahams, R. D. "Does the Pot Melt, Boil, or Brew? Black Children and White Assessment Procedures." *Journal of School Psychology*, 1973, *11* (4), 330-340.

Hartigan, J., and Wigdor, A. K. *Fairness in Employment Testing: Validity Generalization, Minority Issues, and the General Aptitude Test Battery*. Washington, D.C.: National Academy Press, 1989.

Highwater, J. *The Primal Mind: Vision and Reality in Indian America*. New York: Meridian, 1981.

Labov, W. *A Study of the Non-Standard English of Negro and Puerto Rican Speakers in New York City*. Washington, D.C.: U.S. Government Printing Office, 1968.

Labov, W. "Objectivity and Commitment in Linguistic Science." *Language and Society*, 1972, *11*, 165-201.

McShane, D. "Testing American Natives and Alaskan Natives." Paper presented at Native American hearing of the National Commission on Testing and Public Policy, Albuquerque, N.M., April 1989.

Miller-Jones, D. "Culture and Testing." *American Psychologist*, 1989, *44* (2), 360-366.

Miller-Jones, D. "Differences in Social and Cognitive Information Processing Between High- and Low-Achieving Five-Year-Old Black Children." In J. McAdoo and W. Cross (eds.), *Proceedings of the Fifth Conference on Empirical Research in Black Psychology*. Ithaca, N.Y.: African Studies and Research Center, Cornell University, in press.

National Commission on Testing and Public Policy. *From Gatekeeper to Gateway: Transforming Testing in America*. Boston: National Commission on Testing and Public Policy, 1990.

O'Connor, M. "Aspects of Differential Performance by Minority Students on Standardized Tests." In B. Gifford (ed.), *Test Policy and Test Performance: Education, Language, and Culture*. Boston: Kluwer Academic Press, 1989.

Ogbu, J. "Social Stratification and the Socialization of Competence." *Anthropology and Education Quarterly*, 1979, *10*, 3-20.

Ogbu, J. "Origins of Human Competence: A Cultural Ecology Perspective." *Child Development*, 1981, *52*, 413-429.

Ogbu, J. "A Cultural Ecology of Competence Among Inner-City Blacks." In M. B. Spencer, G. K. Brookings, and W. R. Allen (eds.), *Beginnings: The Social and Affective Development of Black Children*. Hillsdale, N.J.: Erlbaum, 1985.

Ogbu, J. "The Consequence of the American Caste System." In U. Neisser (ed.), *The School Achievement of Minority Children: New Perspectives*. Hillsdale, N.J.: Erlbaum, 1986.

Olmedo, E. L. "Testing and Linguistic Minorities." *American Psychologist*, 1981, *36* (10), 1078-1085.

Omi, M., and Winant, H. *Racial Formation in the United States: From the 1960s to the 1980s*. New York: Routledge & Kegan Paul, 1986.

Padilla, A. "Cultural Considerations: Hispanic-American." In R. Tyler and S. White (eds.), *Testing, Teaching, and Learning: Report of a Conference on Research on Testing*. Washington, D.C.: National Institute of Education, 1979.

Perkins, D. N. *Knowledge as Design*. Hillsdale, N.J.: Erlbaum, 1986.

Tsang, C. L. "Informal Assessment of Asian Americans." In B. Gifford (ed.), *Test Policy and Test Performance: Education, Language, and Culture*. Boston: Kluwer Academic Press, 1989.

Tsang, C. L., and Wing, L. C. *Beyond Angel Island: The Education of Asian Americans.* ERIC/ CUE Urban Diversity Series no. 90, 1985.

"Using Demographic Data for Long-Range Planning: An Interview with Harold Hodgkinson." *Phi Delta Kappan,* Oct. 1988, pp. 166-167.

Valdez, G., and Figueroa, R. *The Nature of Bilingualism and the Nature of Testing: Towards the Development of a Coherent Research Agenda.* Boston: Kluwer Academic Press, 1992.

Vygotsky, L. "The Problem of the Cultural Development of the Child." *Journal of Genetic Psychology,* 1929, *36,* 415-434.

Vygotsky, L. *Mind and Society.* Cambridge, Mass.: Harvard University Press, 1978.

Wideman, J. E. *Philadelphia Fire.* Troy, Mo.: Holt, Rinehart & Winston, 1990.

William, T. S. "Some Issues in the Standardized Testing of Minority Students." *Boston University Journal of Education,* 1983, *165* (2), 192-208.

Williams, F. *Language and Poverty: Perspectives on a Theme.* Chicago: Markham, 1970.

CEASAR L. MCDOWELL *is assistant professor of education, Department of Human Development and Psychology, Harvard Graduate School of Education. He served as a staff member of the National Commission on Testing and Public Policy.*

Program evaluators often use race as an explanatory variable without clearly articulating what race means in an evaluation context.

Reconsidering the Use of Race as an Explanatory Variable in Program Evaluation

James Earl Davis

Racial and ethnic minority groups traditionally have been represented disproportionately as participants in many social programs. Racial groups and race differences between groups, however, are frequently discussed without a clear sense of what race means in a program evaluation. One of the ways program evaluators avoid dealing with the complexities of participants' experiences and social locations is by categorizing and therefore assuming homogeneity of condition. Using the concept of race is often a convenient but limited method of labeling groups of people.

This chapter critically analyzes the use of race as an explanatory construct in program evaluations and represents an attempt to encourage the use of a contextual framework in the identification and analysis of race differences. The practice of identifying race differences by using such traditional comparative analytical frameworks as statistical difference testing is critically examined here. In the first part of this chapter, program theory is discussed, as well as its implications for the evaluation of programs for African Americans and other nondominant groups. The second part examines the use of race and race differences in program evaluation and the problems of generalizing program effects for diverse populations. The third part explores some implications for program evaluation design and analysis. The fourth section offers suggestions for examining whether race is a useful explanatory construct in a given evaluation.

This discussion is relevant to program evaluators who employ comparative research designs using race as a variable. One problem with this

NEW DIRECTIONS FOR PROGRAM EVALUATION, no. 53, Spring 1992 © Jossey-Bass Publishers analytical approach is that it often leads to simplistic, misleading, or inappropriate conclusions about programs and program participants (Wilkinson and King, 1987). Most evaluators have failed to understand fully the meaning of race as a variable and the broader social and political implications of its use with respect to program development, program effects, and the delivery of services to minority populations.

Program Theory and Minority Populations

With the social programs of the Great Society and the War on Poverty came the development of evaluation methods and strategies to assess the effectiveness of these efforts. Most of these programs were targeted toward populations that were considered economically impoverished and socially disenfranchised. An important corollary to the development of evaluation methods has been the knowledge on which these methods and strategies rest. Recent efforts to address the charge that program evaluation is atheoretical include the development of program theory (Bickman, 1990, 1987; Chen, 1989; Chen and Rossi, 1987).

The emergence of program theory is seen as a useful and viable strategy for modeling or articulating how programs should work. Nevertheless, it appears that the target population, which is a significant component of the program evaluation, still receives only a modest amount of attention. Chen and Rossi (1987) argue that program evaluations should be theory-driven and not solely oriented toward research design. Traditionally, we have relied on research design to compensate for our lack of knowledge about the way programs and target populations function. For instance, in the absence of such knowledge, randomization serves as a safety net and as a way of dealing with threats to internal validity. This dependence on design and method often results in program evaluations that employ poor program conceptualization, insensitive measures, and inappropriate generalization of findings. Evaluating the effects of a crime-prevention program on an urban minority neighborhood by using evaluation procedures developed for suburban white neighborhoods could be problematic. In a minority community, the program process and the measures of outcomes must be theoretically meaningful within that context—in other words, high in construct validity for the specific population. Therefore, we must know something about the population where a program resides. Evaluators also have to determine adequately how program characteristics and incentives operate within such a context. For example, a program designed to prevent teenage pregnancy and sexually transmitted diseases may be less effective in some African American communities, where the program's materials and sexual content may be in conflict with pervasive religious values. To develop theoretical perspectives on typical outcome measures, such as attitudes and behaviors, evaluators are compelled to be familiar with nuances and their interactions with the targeted population's characteristics.

Social programs are often viewed as being responsible for failing to produce expected results. Programs, however, including their conceptualization and implementation, are not always the problem. While voices in the evaluation community have been less critical of the role of evaluators and evaluation methods (see Murray, 1983; Murray, 1984), program evaluation as a social enterprise is partly responsible and at the core of the problem.

The larger problem, however, as previously mentioned, is the failure of theory, whether it is broad social science theory or program theory, to adequately explain the behavior and characteristics of the populations served by various social programs. One example of this failure is the evaluation of employment training programs for black men. The general assumption underlying most of these programs has been that black men experience higher rates of unemployment because they lack employment opportunities, and that the lack of opportunities is caused by the lack of marketable skills and appropriate attitudes toward work. Unfortunately, these assumptions do not take account of the differential perceptions of black males' personal worth and values as they are related to motivation and behavior with respect to employment. Most job training programs were developed with inadequate understanding of the target population, and the result has been program evaluations that have reinforced negative stereotypes of African American men. The usefulness of evaluations of programs for homeless people in minority communities has also been limited by the absence of a clear theory of homelessness and by the absence of other programs to address the problem (Rossi, 1989). In short, fundamental issues concerning the targeted population must be considered. Program evaluation is recognized as a source of social science data (Chen and Rossi, 1983), and evaluations are often the medium by which the experiences of program participants are presented and disseminated for public consumption. Hence, valid portrayals of these groups are of paramount importance.

What Is Race in Program Evaluation?

The answer to this question is much more complex than most evaluators think. In evaluation research, it is common to use racial groupings unquestioningly. Unfortunately, the issue of race is usually determined at the technical level of data coding. African Americans are usually identified as a distinctive racial group in this country, and so are Asian Americans and European Americans (Allport, 1954; Gardner, Robey, and Smith, 1985; Myrdal, 1944; Pettigrew, 1980; Scarr, 1988; Wilson, 1976). The use of race, however, is much more loaded, and its evaluation implications are often crucial in terms of decision making and knowledge formation. In an effort to explain different program effects and populations, evaluators use the term *race* in categorizing, but the use of race as a variable in evaluation design and analysis is not always benign. One prevailing erroneous assumption is that evaluators and consumers of program evaluations know what race is and how it is being used.

Increasingly, questions are being raised about contemporary uses of race in evaluation studies, specifically with respect to statistical difference testing between groups designated as races. In evaluation studies, as well as in other social research, race is often used to identify differences among less dominant racial groups. According to Banton (1977), the study of race and race effects has been concerned primarily with how whites have defined other groups as "different" and have maintained and justified those supposed differences.

The classification of different populations on the basis of phenotypic and genotypic criteria is common practice in evaluation research, as well as in general social science research. Evaluators often lack knowledge in biology and genetics, but they often interpret correlates with race on the basis of biogenetic meanings, either implicitly or explicitly. Such practices frequently rule out cultural or economic explanations of race differences, such as income, trust in program personnel, and program delivery. It is important to note that if evaluation results privilege biogenetic meanings over other meanings, then interpretations are informed and influenced in distinct ways. For instance, biogenetic explanations of race may lead to very limited suggestions for policy and program developments, such as the use of sterilization or the abandonment of current social interventions. Conversely, race is also used to refer to distinct cultural patterns or to indicate socioeconomic condition. If race is conceptualized in this manner, however, differential results may be derived, since race, defined as a sociocultural concept, cannot be interpreted independent of its environmental context (Wilkinson and King, 1987). This conception of race reflects variations in life experience, developmental course, social practices, and behavior among people who are embedded in a particular ethnocultural context. Many programs, such as community development initiatives, family support services, and health-related services, are more appropriate for evaluations that associate race more in terms of social and cultural characteristics. Program evaluations that adopt this meaning of race are less rigid in their consequences than evaluations that use strictly biogenetic explanations. Furthermore, policy and program decisions based on these evaluation findings probably are less socially damaging and more responsive to the social and cultural settings of programs.

Race Perceptions in Program Evaluation. The general race perceptions that evaluators bring to the evaluation setting may be misinformed, pejorative, and potentially harmful (Boykin, 1979; Hilliard, 1989). These perceptions influence how evaluators ask questions, design studies, and interpret results. When evaluators' questions about African Americans are framed in terms of the group's perceived dysfunctions, the evaluation outcomes will probably be negative. For example, African American families are often seen as deviant, pathological social organizations unable to fulfill the major responsibilities of socializing their members for productive roles in society (Allen, 1978; Moynihan, 1965; Pettigrew, 1964). Many believe that this "undersocialization" leads to such negative outcomes as low academic achievement, juvenile delinquency, and teenage pregnancy. African American populations traditionally have been viewed in relation to the status, position, and hegemony of dominant groups in this country, and it is often this standard to which African Americans are unjustly held. A plethora of data inform us of the unique and often precarious position of African Americans.

It should be noted, however, that there is a convergence of evidence demonstrating that African Americans are clearly at greater risk than most other populations for negative consequences of life and living in the United States. Poverty is one of these risks, and over one-third of the black populace lives at or near the poverty level. But poverty is most evident among African American single-parent families, and over 50 percent of these families are classified as poor (Jaynes and Williams, 1989). These circumstances are extremely important, given the causal relationship between poverty and oppressive social consequences. Furthermore, evidence indicates that poverty reduces a person's repertoire of available resources for coping with adverse social and economic conditions. Moreover, poverty's concomitant factors (inadequate housing, poor sanitation, crowding) have been implicated in a variety of negative outcomes, such as family violence, poor health, and delinquency (Jaynes and Williams, 1989; Glasgow, 1980; Wilson, 1987).

A careful examination of the literature in evaluation and applied social research would reveal many instances of research based on misconceptions about African American communities. One example can be found in evaluators' analyses of single-parent African American families. The demographics of African American households, as defined by parental status, can best be observed and understood not in juxtaposition to those of traditional nuclear families but in relation to the extended-family structures of nonnuclear households (Hunter and Ensiminger, 1992). We know that African American children are more likely to spend a significant part of their early years in households where both parents are not present and are more likely to reside with an extended-family member (Farley and Allen, 1987). Thus, researchers need to understand the notion of extended family and its particular importance for African American children. Race differences in educational achievement are also explained with the help of attention to contextual information about the experiences and characteristics of racial communities. For instance, we have much evidence that African American children are more likely to live in environments that make them less likely to perceive and embrace the benefits of high educational achievement (Boykin, 1986; Ogbu, 1978). In addition, teachers tend to have lower expectations for African American children, which in turn affects their academic performance (Hale-Benson, 1982; Rist, 1970).

Unfortunately, general race perceptions tend not only to undergird the development of social programs but also to influence the development of program theory. Negative effects such as those cited are often the norm, but more positive or appropriate models do exist for evaluating programs in African American communities. This failure in the development of program theory to explain how programs function is perplexing, given the value of information that tells us what is successful in a particular context. Most often, negative models of achievement in education or negative patterns of family functioning are used. Program evaluators' interpretations may be influenced by their initial assumptions about people who are "different." Misunderstanding of differences makes even the most well-meaning evaluator fall victim to the prevailing pejorative ideas and practices concerning minority and ethnic populations.

Race, Culture, and the Social Context of Evaluation. The contemporary practice of program evaluation occurs within social units and environments; hence, evaluations are likely to be circumscribed and often constrained by social and political structures. With this in mind, we can see that program evaluation becomes a social practice that influences how evaluators construct the social realities of program participants and how they analyze results. Their analyses are affected by their understanding of participants' social and cultural experiences (Hilliard, 1989). In this respect, Richardson (1990) argues that evaluations of programs for culturally diverse populations should not be based on assumptions inherent in a positivist evaluation framework; evaluation should be more sensitive to the nature of the social construction of the programs.

Social programs are complex. Numerous factors influence their operation and produce myriad outcomes, intentional or inadvertent. Race, as devised by evaluators, usually becomes a factor. The use of race has important implications for an evaluation because of general misuse and misconceptions of the term *race*. Given the diverse and often ill-founded orientations toward race, a program evaluation would probably be vulnerable to them. What, then, is the evaluator's role in assessing the impact of programs designed for specific racial groups and interpreting the results of race-comparative program evaluations? Ironically, even with all the uncertainties, the answer to this question about race is rarely clear, and race is not adequately defined by program evaluators.

Culturally relevant and sensitive evaluation models must be utilized if programs in minority communities are to be thoroughly examined. Furthermore, decisions about the cultural appropriateness of an evaluation strategy must be coupled with an acknowledgment of the cultural integrity of such groups as African Americans, whose ability to contribute to the development and evaluation of programs in their communities must be recognized. With similar sentiment, Lincoln (1991) points to a great divide between evaluators and program participants, which often represents misunderstanding, at best, and indifference, at worst: "We might study in a more systematic way the art of dealing with people very different from ourselves. Some of us are on the front lines, but many of us, as educated and middle-class persons, do what we can to avoid mingling with people who are not much like us. We instinctively withdraw from people who do not look like us or talk like us, or live—or want to live—like us" (p. 6).

For evaluators, it is more difficult to talk about and embrace racial and cultural variations, since these variations are usually foreign. Our views of others are also framed by monolithic societal expectations. In short, evaluators must cultivate a multiethnocultural perspective, by which they can recognize and incorporate the experiential differences between and among individuals and groups.

Race Generalizations of Program Evaluation. Evaluators are responsible for presenting findings that involve different racial and ethnic groups. It is important that these findings and their generalizations be ethical, appropriate, and informed. Generalizations about race differences are often put forward without much attention to within-group variation and the influence of particular contexts. Traditionally, most social prevention programs have been conceived from dominant middle-class perspectives, and many of these programs have been implemented in African American communities. Some program evaluators have acknowledged that culturally specific approaches are needed, but there have been few serious efforts to design and evaluate programs that are based on culturally diverse perspectives. The problems of generalizing from nondynamic program models are considerable, and the potential damage to program participants is severe.

House (1990) identifies extreme examples of the racist and sexist assumptions that often preoccupied the work of early social scientists. He quickly adds, however, that contemporary evaluation practices, based on current evaluation methods, are less blatantly unjust and less destructive, because evaluators' assumptions start at "higher plateaus of moral sensitivity" (p. 25). While it is true that contemporary evaluations are not as crude, the potential effects on the unempowered groups that programs are intended to aid can still be quite damaging.

Another problem is that frequently social programs are developed to address problems for particular groups or organizations and then implemented for other groups that are not appropriate targets. Mismatches of programs and populations often lead to erroneous findings. For instance, early evaluations of Head Start found that the program actually had negative effects on children. These anomalous findings were partly due to the inadequate and inappropriate measures used with Head Start families that represented a variety of racial and ethnic groups not completely captured by standardized measurement instruments (Grimmett and Garrett, 1989; Laosa, 1982). Again, the knowledge of the program population was limited, and so models conceived for program evaluation, based on the behavior and experience of other groups, were inapplicable.

Many evaluations of such programs as Head Start, Follow Through, PUSH/Excel, and CETA were carried out with predominantly African American program participants (Farrar and House, 1983; House, Glass, McLean, and Walker, 1978); thus, evaluation outcomes had differential ramifications for the communities of these participants. In the recent evaluation literature, reconceptualization of program evaluation is being promoted in order to provide protection for these communities and rectify injustices in practice that may be blatant or unanticipated (House, 1988; Lincoln, 1991; Richardson, 1990). The question remains, however: How do we conceptualize program evaluation in ways that maintain the integrity of racial and ethnic groups? An argument can be made that we must start by reexamining our ideas and assumptions about the populations that are often the targets of social programs and policies.

Implications for Evaluation Design and Data Analysis

There appear to be connections between traditional methods of measuring program outcomes and the representation of race differences in performance and other outcome measures. Methods are not adequate substitutes for informed analysis and substantively grounded judgment. Traditional strategies of determining program effects (for example, analysis of covariance, or ANCOVA) are given too much weight in providing information on how to think about race and race variations. Looking for statistical differences between groups designated by race is usually a questionable enterprise, if it is the sole means of determining differences (Zuckerman, 1990; Lynn, 1989). Carver (1978) argues for the use of other scientific methods for examining data and replicating results, rather than looking to statistical difference testing to provide information about groups.

While statistical analyses used in program evaluations have become increasingly sophisticated, our ability to use them in ways that produce sound findings about program effects has not advanced to the same level. Expectations of what our evaluation methods can yield may be too lofty. Nevertheless, the use of personal judgment and experience in designing, analyzing, and interpreting evaluation results with respect to racial differences is believed to be far superior in comprehending the complex social phenomena that are the focus of evaluation studies (Einhorn and Hogarth, 1986).

Judgment in program evaluation plays a significant role in the assessment of treatment effects, particularly in quasi-experimentation (Cordray, 1986). Many early efforts in quasi-experimentation were impoverished in their notions of what constituted program effectiveness. These "black box" approaches did not allow for the incorporation of information about how programs work and how programs interact with different populations. In these approaches, the program was seen as sufficient to produce its intended outcome. The subtleties of programs and how they are affected by contextual factors were absent from this static evaluation model. In this model, program effectiveness was typically determined by the relative performance of the treatment group by comparison with the control group. Thus, tests of statistical differences provided much of the evidence for program effectiveness.

Data-analytical techniques should not completely replace informed program analysis based on knowledge obtained in the context of program participants' lives and experience. An enormous amount of information about the location and contexts of programs is missing from the discussion of programs' causal claims. Often, knowledge of a program's clientele and the program's appropriateness for its environment is needed to advance thinking about the program's causal assertions. Unfortunately for African Americans and other U.S. racial minorities, this information is, at best, partially known but discarded or, at worst, not known or even cared about. This is not to say that experimental and quasi-experimental studies are not useful for program evaluation; to the contrary. These methods are very powerful in revealing program effects, but results must be examined more carefully, and with sensitivity to diverse populations.

A comparative analytical approach works from the assumption that because African Americans are homogeneous in their condition and experience, programs are homogeneous in their effects. There is relatively little information about the many sources of variation within the black population. African Americans are the largest racial minority in this country, but much within-group variation and in-depth understanding will be completely lost with traditional race-comparative analysis in program evaluation. The following section discusses ways for evaluators to be more responsive to the complexities of race in their work.

Conducting Race-Sensitive Evaluations

Common strategies are available for evaluators to examine whether race is a useful explanatory construct in particular evaluations. While there is no panacea to rid all program evaluations of their biases, the following suggestions may help ensure appropriate evaluation results and interpretations when race is used as a variable. These practices are not exhaustive; they are part of a larger effort to produce more effective evaluations sensitive to race.

Within- and Between-Group Comparisons. Analyze whether differences between identified racial groups are also common within those same groups. Differences between racial groups are often overemphasized, while important variations within groups are dismissed. For instance, differences among urban and rural African American families account for much of what appears to be cross-race difference, yet they are rarely stressed.

Culturally Sensitive Evaluators. Evaluation teams consisting of members of the minority communities where the evaluations are based would provide more of the cultural sensitivity needed to produce useful evaluations. This is particularly important when race variables are culturally defined.

Feedback of Evaluation Interpretations. Before evaluation results are disseminated, feedback concerning race effects and differences is crucial. Bias and inaccuracies in evaluation interpretations may be detected by members of racial and ethnic groups.

Contextual Analysis of the Program. Information about the social location of a program can inform evaluation results and interpretations. Of primary importance is how a program's context directs evaluators to appropriate meanings of race. When race is viewed as a social or cultural construct, its definition is usually context-specific. Therefore, differences in the race variable emerge at the program site.

Evaluation Variable Exchange. Exchange different conceptual meanings of race to see whether evaluation interpretations are affected. This is a way to validate the conceptual appropriateness of race as an explanatory variable. Does conceptualizing race as a biogenetic variable change the interpretation of a preschool compensatory education evaluation that demonstrates no program effects on the academic achievement of African American children?

Race should not always be of major concern in an evaluation, but a preoccupation with it often masks the significance of such variables as socioeconomic condition. Traditionally, there has been a willingness on the part of program evaluators to use race as a proxy variable for actual causal variables, such as poverty, unemployment, and family structure. Evaluators must be more inclined to investigate the poor and the social conditions and cultural responses to poverty, not just racial categorizations, which often provide merely superficial analyses.

Conclusion

As more African Americans are trained as evaluators and social researchers, some of the issues mentioned in this discussion will be addressed, but the onus of correction should not be placed on minority evaluators. Who, then, should be responsible for evaluations in African American and other minority communities? There is still considerable disagreement on this issue. Vestiges of a view popular among black social scientists during the late 1960s and early 1970s continue to be expressed when we hear that the special insight of black researchers renders them best qualified to conduct program evaluations in black communities. To the contrary, any competent evaluator, African American or not, should have the ability and perspective to conduct a careful and sensitive analysis of race differences, as well as a competent assessment of programs in African American environments. Evaluators should be most thoughtful about the definitions used and should be especially sensitive to the bias of untested assumptions, which often become part of evaluation findings. Evaluators should also supply supporting evidence for the choices they make.

Program evaluation does not take place in a social and political vacuum. Program evaluators who use race as a variable must understand and appreciate the environmental context of this amorphous, value-laden concept. What is most important, however, is how evaluators react after race differences or race effects are discovered. What takes place at this juncture is of critical importance, not only because responses may be politically driven or socially determined but also because the integrity of program evaluation as a profession is at stake. Program evaluators are obligated to be fair and equitable in their constructions of race and as accurate as possible in their analyses of race effects and differences. This does not mean overlooking race differences because of potential political controversy; evaluators have a responsibility to clearly define the meanings of race in their work and to understand the ramifications of those meanings. Program evaluation, as an important social enterprise, needs to become more self-critical and to redefine itself and its ways of knowing those it seeks to serve.

References

Allen, W. "The Search for Applicable Theories of Black Family Life." *Journal of Marriage and the Family*, 1978, *40*, 111–129.

Allport, G. W. *The Nature of Prejudice*. Reading, Mass.: Addison-Wesley, 1954.

Banton, A. *The Idea of Race*. London: Tavistock, 1977.

Bickman, L. "The Functions of Program Theory." In L. Bickman (ed.), *Using Program Theory in Evaluation*. New Directions for Program Evaluation, no. 33. San Francisco: Jossey-Bass, 1987.

Bickman, L. (ed.). *Advances in Program Theory*. New Directions for Program Evaluation, no. 47. San Francisco: Jossey-Bass, 1990.

Boykin, A. W. "Black Psychology and the Research Process: Keeping the Baby But Throwing Out the Bath Water." In A. Boykin, A. Franklin, and J. Yates (eds.), *Research Directions of Black Psychology*. New York: Russell Sage Foundation, 1979.

Boykin, A. W. "The Triple Quandary and the Schooling of Afro-American Children." In U. Neisser (ed.), *The School Achievement of Minority Children: New Perspectives*. Hillsdale, N.J.: Erlbaum, 1986.

Bryk, A. S., and Raudenbush, S. "The Potential Contribution of Program Evaluation to Social Problem Solving." In A. Bryk (ed.), *Stakeholder-Based Evaluation*. New Directions for Program Evaluation, no. 17. San Francisco: Jossey-Bass, 1983.

Carver, R. P. "The Case Against Statistical Significance Testing." *Harvard Educational Review*, 1978, *34*, 386–400.

Chen, H. T. *Sensible Evaluation: The Theory-Driven Approach.* Newbury Park, Calif.: Sage, 1989.

Chen, H. T., and Rossi, P. "Evaluating with Sense: The Theory-Driven Approach." *Evaluation Review*, 1983, *7*, 283–302.

Chen, H. T., and Rossi, P. "The Theory-Driven Approach to Validity." *Evaluation and Program Planning*, 1987, *10*, 95–103.

Cordray, D. S. "Quasi-Experimental Analysis: A Mixture of Methods and Judgment." In W. Trochim (ed.), *Advances in Quasi-Experimental Design and Analysis.* New Directions for Program Evaluation, no. 31. San Francisco: Jossey-Bass, 1986.

Einhorn, H. J., and Hogarth, R. M. "Judging Probable Cause." *Psychological Bulletin*, 1986, *99*, 3–19.

Farley, R., and Allen, W. *The Color Line and the Quality of American Life.* New York: Russell Sage Foundation, 1987.

Farrar, E., and House, E. R. "The Evaluation of PUSH/Excel: A Case Study." In A. Bryk (ed.), *Stakeholder-Based Evaluation.* New Directions for Program Evaluation, no. 17. San Francisco: Jossey-Bass, 1983.

Gardner, J. W., Robey, B., and Smith, P. C. *Asian Americans: Growth, Change, and Diversity.* Washington, D.C.: Population Reference Bureau, 1985.

Glasgow, D. G. *The Black Underclass: Poverty, Unemployment, and Entrapment of Ghetto Youth.* San Francisco: Jossey-Bass, 1980.

Grimmett, S., and Garrett, A. M. "A Review of Evaluations of Project Head Start." *Journal of Negro Education*, 1989, *58*, 30–38.

Hale-Benson, J. E. *Black Children: Their Roots, Culture, and Learning Styles.* Baltimore: Johns Hopkins University Press, 1982.

Hilliard, A. G., III. "Kemetic (Egyptian) Historical Revision: Implications for Cross-Cultural Evaluation and Research in Education." *Evaluation Practice*, 1989, *10*, 7–23.

House, E. R. *Jesse Jackson and the Politics of Charisma: The Rise and Fall of the PUSH/Excel Program.* Boulder, Colo.: Westview Press, 1988.

House, E. R. "Methodology and Justice." In K. Sirotnik (ed.), *Evaluation and Social Justice: Issues in Public Education.* New Directions for Program Evaluation, no. 45. San Francisco: Jossey-Bass, 1990.

House, E. R., Glass, G. V., McLean, L., and Walker, D. "No Simple Answer: A Critique of the Follow Through Evaluation." *Harvard Educational Review*, 1978, *48*, 128–160.

Hunter, A. G., and Ensiminger, M. "The Diversity and Fluidity of Children's Living Arrangements: Life Course and Family Transitions in an Urban Afro-American Community." *Journal of Marriage and the Family*, 1992, *54*, 239–248.

Jaynes, G. D., and Williams, R. M. (eds.). *A Common Destiny: Blacks and American Society.* Washington, D.C.: National Academy Press, 1989.

Laosa, L. "The Sociocultural Context of Evaluation." In B. Spodek (ed.), *Handbook of Research in Early Childhood Education.* New York: Free Press, 1982.

Lincoln, Y. S. "The Arts and Sciences of Program Evaluation." *Evaluation Practice*, 1991, *12*, 1–7.

Lynn, M. "Criticisms of an Evolutionary Hypothesis About Race Differences." *Journal of Research in Personality*, 1989, *23*, 21–34.

Moynihan, D. P. *The Negro Family: The Case for National Action.* Washington, D.C.: U.S. Government Printing Office, 1965.

Murray, C. A. "Stakeholders as Deck Chairs." In A. Bryk (ed.), *Stakeholder-Based Evaluation.* New Directions for Program Evaluation, no. 17. San Francisco: Jossey-Bass, 1983.

Murray, C. A. *Losing Ground: American Social Policy, 1950–1980.* New York: Basic Books, 1984.

Myrdal, G. *An American Dilemma.* New York: HarperCollins, 1944.

Ogbu, J. U. *Minority Status and Caste: The American System in Cross-Cultural Perspective.* San Diego, Calif.: Academic Press, 1978.

Pettigrew, T. *A Profile of the Negro American.* New York: Van Nostrand Reinhold, 1964.

Pettigrew, T. (ed.). *The Sociology of Race Relations: Reflection and Reform.* New York: Free Press, 1980.

Richardson, V. "At-Risk Programs: Evaluation and Critical Inquiry." In K. Sirotnik (ed.), *Evaluation and Social Justice: Issues in Public Education.* New Directions for Program Evaluation, no. 45. San Francisco: Jossey-Bass, 1990.

Rist, R. "Student Social Class and Teacher Expectations: The Self-Fulfilling Prophecy in Ghetto Education." *Harvard Educational Review,* 1970, 40, 411–451.

Rossi, P. H. *Down and Out in America: The Origins of Homelessness.* Chicago: University of Chicago Press, 1989.

Scarr, S. "Race and Gender as Psychological Variables." *American Psychologist,* 1988, 43, 56–59.

Wilkinson, D. Y., and King, G. "Conceptual and Methodological Issues in the Use of Race as a Variable: Policy Implications." *Milbank Quarterly,* 1987, 65, 57–71.

Wilson, W. J. *Power, Racism, and Privilege: Race Relations in Theoretical and Sociohistorical Perspectives.* New York: Free Press, 1976.

Wilson, W. J. *The Truly Disadvantaged: The Inner City, the Underclass, and Public Policy.* Chicago: University of Chicago Press, 1987.

Zuckerman, M. "Some Dubious Premises in Research and Theory on Racial Differences." *American Psychologist,* 1990, 45, 1297–1303.

JAMES EARL DAVIS is assistant professor in the Department of Educational Studies, University of Delaware, Newark.

Issues for program evaluation are raised through an analysis of previous integrative research in multicultural teacher education.

Synthesizing Research in Multicultural Teacher Education: Findings and Issues for Evaluation of Cultural Diversity

Jeffrey S. Beaudry

Between 1972 and 1991, new curricula in multicultural education were adopted in Iowa, Minnesota, Oregon, Georgia, New York, and California (Willis, 1990). Recently published social studies syllabi from the state education departments have espoused multicultural education as a new direction for curriculum design and evaluation, one intent on dealing with minority issues. These curriculum changes represent a clear legacy of the social change agenda of the 1960s and a renewal of emphasis on the value of cultural diversity—the "curriculum of inclusion," as it has been called.

At the least, program evaluators can expect to be involved in formative evaluation of pilot programs in school districts, examination of instructional materials to verify accuracy and bias of content, assessment of tests and testing procedures to identify biases, observation of learning environments and classrooms to better understanding of the implications of multicultural education for teachers and learners, and study of the outcomes and effects of these curricular changes. In facing these tasks, program evaluators need to consider the principles of multicultural inclusion and be sensitive to minority issues in the evaluation process; that is, the program planning, implementation, and evaluation process must seek to include the multiple perspectives of ethnicity, race, gender, and social class. There are also claims that disabled populations should be represented (Grant and Sleeter, 1989). Much of the discussion of stakeholder-focused evaluation has covered similar ground, using the term *client* as a proxy for inclusion, as in Gill and Zimmerman's evaluation (1990) of racial/ethnic and gender bias in the Michigan court system. The stakeholder approach represents a significant step toward multicultural representation and participation in program design and evaluation research (House, 1991; Weiss, 1991).

This chapter concentrates on the body of research that has addressed the issue of improving education through programs and courses in multicultural teacher education. My experiences in working on an evaluation of a multicultural teacher education program (Beaudry, 1990) and my interest in research synthesis prompted a thorough examination of issues and existing research in the field. So far, there has not been a meta-analysis of research published in the field of multicultural education. This leaves many questions unanswered about the availability of research, the development of program theory and explanatory models, the direction of program effects, the quality of research, mediating variables, and who is doing the research.

There are two major themes in this chapter. The first is that multicultural issues are closely related to minority issues. Multicultural theory may play a major role in the development of descriptive models for understanding the processes through which individuals and minority groups attain more in-depth, rewarding participation in our society. Minority issues reflect the ongoing need to address racism, sexism, social-class bias, and other forms of bias. The second theme is that while meta-analysis of multicultural education may represent a certain level of scientific maturity in the field, it must be approached with an understanding of the findings and questions raised by researchers who have studied the interaction of key variables—ethnicity, race, gender, and social class.

This chapter is organized around the following topics:

1. Background of minority issues and definitions of multicultural education, and the debate over the value of multicultural education and minority issues
2. Examination of selected primary research articles in multicultural teacher education, to further observe factors and effects considered to be significant
3. Comparison of narrative and integrative research-review approaches, with examples of integrative reviews of multicultural teacher education
4. Issues for research syntheses and meta-analysis in multicultural education, with examples of meta-analyses in bilingual education and examples of the effects of examiner familiarity on black, Caucasian, and Hispanic children
5. Qualitative research-synthesis techniques
6. Why knowledge of multicultural education is worthwhile for addressing minority issues, with recommendations for program evaluators doing multicultural evaluation.

Minority Issues and Multicultural Education

There is a need to understand the relationship between minority issues and multicultural education.

Background of Minority Issues. After the precedent-setting actions of the Supreme Court in the *Brown v. Board of Education* decision in 1954 and the funding from the 1964 Civil Rights Act, social scientists began to focus on measuring the differential effects of schooling. In the landmark report by Coleman and others (1966), the powerful effects of the home, parents' background, and socioeconomic status were shown to supersede the effects of schools' resources, curriculum, quality of teachers, and background of fellow students in predicting achievement. These findings ignited further debate over the practical implications of equal educational opportunity for schooling and for evaluation, a controversy that remains unsettled to this day (Coleman, 1990).

At the heart of the sociological analysis of this controversy are ethnicity, race, gender, and social-class concepts. These familiar yet elusive descriptors of human differences have to be defined (see Rothenburg, 1988). *Race* is a term used to categorize hereditary characteristics; *racism* entails the subordination of one racial group by another. In contrast, *ethnic groupings* relate to social, cultural, and linguistic ties (Allport, 1958); negative prejudice toward ethnic groups may be mistakenly called *racism*. *Gender differences* seem obvious: sexism almost always concerns the oppression of women by men but also includes social and psychological microinequities (Campbell, 1989), subtle factors militating against women's full participation in society. *Social-class differentiation* in the United States is primarily related to economic factors, such as wealth and income, but may also be associated with geographical factors. Without critical analysis of the interactions of these variables, program evaluators may be working with, masking, and even fostering misconceptions, stereotypes, and biases emanating from these phenomena.

Minorities, especially African Americans and language-different minorities, have long felt the dominant culture's hegemony through labels like *culturally disadvantaged, educationally disadvantaged,* and *at risk* (Anyon, 1981; Giroux, 1981; Pallas, Natriello, and McDill, 1989). Five empirically derived indicators connected with being educationally disadvantaged are "minority racial/ethnic group identity, living in a poverty household, living in a single-parent family, having a poorly educated mother, and having a non-English-language background" (Pallas, Natriello, and McDill, 1989, p. 17).

For black Americans, Hispanic Americans, Native Americans, and Chicanos, investment in social programs has yielded only modest changes in equality of educational and occupational opportunity. For example, the dropout rate for black and Hispanic youth remains higher than for white children (Pallas, Natriello, and McDill, 1989). In school governance, fewer than 5 percent of the people elected to school boards are from minorities, and only 36 percent of those elected are women (Institute for Educational Leadership, 1986). Coleman (1990) describes another pattern of inequity, based on interactions of race/ethnicity and geographical location, sometimes used as a proxy for social class in comparing white and black achievement: "The comparison with whites in the rural South shows the groups beginning near the same point in the first grade, and diverging over the years of school. The comparison with blacks in the Northeast shows the two groups beginning further apart at the first grade and remaining about the same distance apart. The comparison with blacks in the rural South shows the two groups beginning far apart and moving much farther apart over the years of school" (p. 27). One consequence of the lack of educational opportunity is its effects on occupational opportunity.

It is not that there is no need for minorities to enter the professions (Darling-Hammond, 1989); on the contrary. As we enter the 1990s, there remains a serious long-term predicament for education: the discontinuity between teacher and student diversity (Grant and Secada, 1989). Schools can be characterized as having predominantly white teachers and administrators and a growing percentage of culturally diverse students. This discontinuity is exacerbated in urban education and at other levels of education (for example, in graduate school enrollment and in university faculties). The lack of available talent is acute in highly specialized professions like engineering, medicine, and, of course, program evaluation. In effect, minority groups have been the objects of study (the problem), rarely asking the questions or guiding or actually conducting evaluations (the solution).

By the late 1960s, as historical patterns of separation began to give way to mandated integration, an understanding of how prejudicial attitudes, both positive and negative, might shape communities', schools', and individuals' responses to these changes was still being developed. Allport (1958) wrote that, given group norms and values concerning prejudice and social distance, it was unlikely that attempts to change individuals' attitudes would be effective. Other, competing views have been advanced by theorists of the social and environmental determinants of prejudice and discrimination. What has happened in the development of theories, and in evaluation research in the United States, to support or contradict these views on the interactions of race, ethnicity, gender, and social class with respect to multicultural education and minority issues?

Multicultural Education Defined. Multicultural education has emerged as a conceptual framework for curriculum inquiry, curriculum development, and evaluation. Banks (1988) has pointed out the need not only to change individuals' prejudicial attitudes and behavior but also to focus on the social structure of the institution of school—its norms, power relationships, attitudes toward minority languages, and variables contributing to the hidden values that have significant impacts on students, teachers, and staff.

Textbooks on multicultural education began appearing in the 1970s and are now being published at an increasing rate. A sample includes Klassen and Gollnick (1977), Colangelo, Dustin, and Foxley (1985), Rothenburg (1988), Bennett and LeCompte (1990), and Pai (1990). Banks (1988) offers the following definition of multicultural education: "Multicultural education suggests a type of education concerned with creating educational environments in which students from a variety of microcultural groups—such as race/ethnicity, gender, social class, regional groups, and handicapped persons—experience educational equality" (pp. 79–80). Such concepts as prejudice, discrimination, identity conflicts, and marginalization are assumed to affect the whole spectrum of such groups. Bennett and LeCompte (1990) describe multicultural education as "an approach to teaching and learning that is based upon democratic values and beliefs and seeks to foster cultural pluralism within culturally diverse societies and an interdependent world. . . . Cultural plurality is an ideal state of societal conditions characterized by equity and mutual respect among existing cultural groups" (p. 11). This definition reflects the assumption that ethnic and cultural groups should be permitted to retain cultural identity while coexisting with the whole society. In addition, gender and social-class issues must be represented in the design and evaluation of programs.

Research in Multicultural Teacher Education

In the 1960s and 1970s, the first research studies were initiated that examined specific programs in multicultural teacher education.

Primary Research Findings. Evaluation research studies in multicultural teacher education have focused on preservice and inservice teacher education programs (appropriate settings for addressing multicultural education issues). Fewer studies are available on the recruitment strategies of minorities into the teaching profession (Grant and Secada, 1989). Outcome measures have typically assessed the immediate program effects on multicultural knowledge and attitudes toward racial/ethnic groups. While gains in multicultural knowledge are consistently positive and remain stable in follow-up measures, negative prejudicial attitudes toward gender and ethnicity have a tendency to return a month after the program (Hennington, 1981). Grant and Grant (1985) found that bias toward social class was the most difficult barrier to overcome in a workshop setting.

From this research, three familiar types of program designs have emerged: workshops of from one day to two weeks in length (Baker, 1973; Hennington, 1981); courses in the undergraduate curriculum, taught on campus, sometimes in conjunction with or followed by field experiences (Grant, 1981; Ladson-Billings, 1991); and undergraduate courses taught at off-campus sites, immersing students in particular cultures for two to four months (Mahan, 1982; Noordhoff and Kleinfeld, 1991).

The greatest change in behavior has been reported in connection with programs using cultural immersion to prepare teachers for diversity. Mahan (1982) placed 291 primarily Anglo students on a Hopi Indian reservation with Hopi cooperating teachers and supervisors. Noordhoff and Kleinfeld (1991) report long-term experiences in Alaska in isolated Eskimo and Native American communities. Outcomes have included multicultural knowledge and attitudes, as well as measures of the employment success of project participants in culturally diverse settings and acceptance of student teachers by school principals (Mahan, 1982). In both aspects, program effects have been extremely positive. Typical field experiences for preservice teachers are related to cultural-immersion models, but it is unlikely that such models will be widely adopted. The strong effects of this program design underscore the power of combining experience and education (Dewey, 1938), as well as the contributions of diverse groups to planning and implementation.

For teachers, constraints on adopting multicultural education practices are related to individual, demographic, and institutional factors. A number of studies have indicated resistance to change on the part of teachers who "were teaching in predominantly white classrooms and therefore did not see a reason to use multicultural education" (Grant and Secada, 1989, p. 410). This finding is confirmed by Baty (1972) and Washington (1981), who have reported that minority teachers, more experienced teachers, and teachers in culturally diverse schools were more likely to value multicultural attitudes and knowledge and implement multicultural teaching practices. Clear descriptions of multicultural teaching practices are limited in the research but are becoming available (see Grant and Sleeter, 1989). Another problem for education in particular is the finding that students in education programs have scored lower on tests of multicultural knowledge than students in other undergraduate majors (Ladson-Billings, 1991).

Support has been lacking from institutions, a finding based on qualitative studies. Similar findings have been reported in national data sets relying on path analysis and hierarchical linear modeling (Barrington and Hendricks, 1989; Bryk and Thum, 1989). In effect, program designers have been able to disseminate knowledge but seem to have had less impact on teachers' classroom behavior, a finding consistent for preservice and inservice teachers. Preservice students have reported that their cooperating teachers were too busy to add new, multicultural instructional materials. Practicing teachers have claimed that changes to incorporate multicultural education into practice would not be made without visible and vocal support from principals and administrators.

This lack of support touches on subtle institutional resistance to change in curricula and in instruction. I am involved in a study examining the influence of institutional environments on Cummins's framework for the empowerment of students in kindergarten bilingual education programs (Warshaw, Olson, and Beaudry, 1991). This study is based on qualitative research methods and has found the anticipated pattern of institutional resistance to bilingual education. We are seeking to identify significant factors that may facilitate or constrain bilingual education programs, a task that may assist in operationalizing variables for larger-scale quantitative studies of multicultural education.

Instrumentation Used in Multicultural Education Research. Since evaluation outcomes for multicultural education programs have typically focused on changes in the attitudes and knowledge of participants, how have these changes been measured and quantified? There are standardized, pencil-and-paper instruments available to measure attitudes. Miller (1991) lists instruments culled from surveys of political attitudes, as well as a number of surveys of sociometric preference, like Bogardus's Social Distance Scale. I worked recently on an evaluation of the Teacher Opportunity Corps (TOC). The goal of TOC was to recruit minority students into the teaching profession. Students, professors, school principals, and TOC staff were interviewed, and participant observation was used to document and describe TOC activities (Beaudry, 1990). Students have responded to standardized survey instruments, including the Coopersmith Self-Esteem Inventory, Schutz's Val-Ed Survey (FIRO) and FIRO-B awareness scales, and the Dunn, Dunn, and Price Learning Styles Inventory. We recently used a survey instrument described by Larke and McJamerson (1990) to measure changes in students' attitudes on issues related to the content of a course in multicultural education. Results of these evaluations are still being analyzed.

There are also newly developed measures of multicultural attitudes and knowledge, some specifically designed for education, such as the Multi-Factor Attitude Inventory, the Multicultural Education Survey, the Ethnic History and Cultural Awareness Survey, the Desire to Teach Minority Children Survey, and the Multicultural Teaching Scale (Contreras, 1988; Wayson, 1988). I have found little reporting about the validity and reliability of these instruments, a fact that points to the need for further research. While most of these instruments assess the attitudes and knowledge of teachers, I have yet to find a survey that uses students' perceptions of the social-psychological classroom environment to evaluate program effectiveness, as suggested by Haertel and Walberg (1988). They estimate that measurement of classroom environment has accounted for 13 percent to 46 percent of variance on cognitive, affective, and behavioral criteria, a robust indicator that could be useful in measuring classroom dimensions of multicultural education.

School districts, especially those with large concentrations of minority groups, may be too immersed in program operations or too understaffed or underprepared to collect reliable data. There may be reluctance to release cultural and ethnic data for analysis, given the fear that the data may be used to criticize these groups. The fear of the abuse of data is a concern that I have encountered on more than one occasion. To strengthen the involvement of schools in the evaluation process, O'Sullivan (1990) has proposed a developmental approach that may help evaluators overcome such problems.

Research Reviews of Multicultural Teacher Education

In addition to single research studies, literature reviewers can systematically evaluate and integrate past research (Light and Pillemer, 1984).

Types of Research Reviews. In addition to single research studies, literature reviewers can systematically evaluate and integrate past research (Light and Pillemer, 1984). Cooper (1989) identifies two types of literature review: integrative research review and theoretical review. The integrative review is designed to be thorough and unbiased in the collection, inclusion, and analysis of research articles. The integrative review may employ some technique of quantification to assess the outcomes of each study, such as vote counting or meta-analysis. Slavin (1987) has proposed a modification of these, called the *best-evidence synthesis*, which combines features of meta-analysis and narrative reviews and provides for strict selection criteria to eliminate methodologically unsound studies (1987). The theoretical, or narrative, review tends to be less systematic and biased and more selective in choosing what evidence is evaluated. It emphasizes the author's conceptualization of the topic. The theoretical review may be a historical review or a narrative review based on the author's choice of significant research. There is usually no clear methodological claim to searching or evaluating the literature.

Findings from Reviews. In the field of multicultural teacher education, I have identified five reviews of research so far that claim to integrate the topics of ethnicity, race, gender, and social class. All these reviews use the term *multicultural* or *multiethnic* to identify the area of interest. Gay's narrative (1983) is important because it establishes a firm argument for the existence of cultural bias in curricular and instructional materials. In the review by Grant and Sleeter (1986), separate categories of ethnicity, race, gender, and social class are used to analyze "a sample of education literature from four education journals, spanning ten years, to determine the extent to which status groups were integrated" (p. 195). Their findings are that race issues, especially research in changing prejudicial attitudes, are most widely represented in the literature and that gender and social class are most often left as issues that are not integrated into the studies.

The only quantitative analysis of the field of multicultural education was done by Sleeter and Grant (1987). It includes analysis of eighty-nine articles and thirty-nine books. They sorted the literature into five educational approaches: teaching the culturally different child, a human relations approach, single-group studies (for example, African American studies), multicultural education, and education that is multicultural and social reconstructionist (Grant and Sleeter, 1986). A vote-count procedure was used to rate the outcomes of the ten empirically based research articles. Sleeter and Grant found that 90 percent of the studies measured changes in attitudes, particularly negative prejudice toward minority racial and ethnic groups. Measures of multicultural knowledge were examined in 30 percent of the studies, while teachers' behavior was examined in 20 percent of the studies. Of the measured outcomes, 50 percent showed improvement and 50 percent showed mixed results immediately after coursework. In measures of follow-up results, changes in knowledge and changes in attitudes were reversed and showed a decline to original, preprogram levels.

In their review of multicultural teacher education, Grant and Secada (1989) have identified studies examining the effects of multicultural education on preservice education and inservice teacher education programs. Of these studies, sixteen focused on preservice education and seven looked at inservice teacher education. According to Grant and Secada, "Six studies used a pretest/posttest design; the others used a posttest only" (p. 413). In some of the studies, "posttest only" meant using openended interviews of teachers and student teachers and observations of classrooms and field experiences. Analysis of the studies was mainly descriptive and was accompanied by comments about positive and mixed results. Some of their findings are that length and intensity of the program were positively correlated with increasing multicultural knowledge and changing attitudes, that courses were more effective than workshops, and that two or more courses (especially combined with field experiences) were more effective than just one. Using the vote-count method, I have estimated that 52 percent of the studies of preservice program outcomes were positive, and approximately 42 percent of the inservice results were positive. These findings are similar to those of Sleeter (1985) and indicate the difficulty of achieving consistent, long-term positive results.

There were a number of themes in these reviews, above all the continuing need to provide an integrative approach to studying interactions of race/ethnicity, gender, and social class. Omitting any of these variables may confound a study's external and construct validity. There was repeated attention to the poor descriptions of program implementation (an issue of construct and internal validity). Reviewers all commented on the modest to low size of the effects of multicultural teacher education. Using Walberg's (1984) research on the estimation of effect sizes from vote counts, an estimate of effects based on approximately 50 percent positive findings would place the overall effect size for multicultural education near zero. This estimate could be refined with more exact meta-analytical techniques. It does bring immediate questions to mind—it may be a result of the counterbalance of short-term versus long-term program effects—as well as questions about the direction of the nonsignificant findings. What about the differential effects for different racial and ethnic groups? Can these effects be isolated? The questions about instrumentation and the finding of little or no statistical difference are issues of statistical conclusion validity.

We need more explicit models of multicultural education theory. For example, what are the hypothetical relationships of prejudice, attitudes, knowledge, classroom performance, and measures of institutional support? Is there a causal order for the essential constructs? The breadth of studies in this area is remarkable, with reports of school-based and off-campus cultural-immersion programs. At the same time, synthesis of the research seems to be in the early stages. Attempts to use vote counting have brought some rigor to the reviews. The next step requires even more explicit analysis of the research.

Issues for Meta-Analysis Research

One tool that has contributed to the assessment of research and program effectiveness is quantitative synthesis, or meta-analysis (Glass, Smith, and McGaw, 1981; Rosenthal, 1984; Hedges and Olkin, 1985; Hunter and Schmidt, 1991). The primary advantage of meta-analysis is that it not only "statistically summarizes the effects reported by primary research studies but also provides detailed, replicable rationales and descriptions of literature searches, selection of primary studies, metrics of study effects, statistical procedures, and overall results, as well as the results that are exceptional with respect to their context or to their sample of subjects" (Carlberg and Walberg, 1984, p. 11). As a technique, meta-analysis has inspired both acceptance and controversy in the field of program evaluation and research.

The reliability and stability of effect-size estimates must be evaluated to correct for bias due to heterogeneity of variances and to account for mediating variables. Effect-size estimates must be examined to identify the confounding effects of quality of research design, sample size, type of treatment and program design (to include subject matter as well as alterable program variables), composition of groups (to include ethnicity, race, social class, and such sampling characteristics as preservice and inservice status of teachers), and methodological considerations (location of treatment, instrumentation, mortality of treatment, and control groups). With testing of the adequacy of data, for goodness of fit and for specification of regression models, validity and reliability of results in a meta-analysis of multicultural teacher education may be more rigorously examined (Hedges and Olkin, 1985; Hunter and Schmidt, 1989). Assessment of reliability helps in evaluating the stability of effect-size estimates across a variety of conditions and ultimately assists in the development of indicators for what should be expected of programs in this area. Further critique of the problems of specifying inclusion criteria, coding, the effects of Type I and Type II errors, and the dilemma of combining between- and within-study findings in the implementation of meta-analysis can be found in Abrami, Cohen, and d'Appollonia (1988). In essence, should meta-analysts retain effect sizes for individual program effects, or should effect sizes be weighted, or aggregated, for each study?

Some general issues for meta-analysis focus on the design of experimental studies and the types of validity—internal, statistical-conclusion, construct, and external (Cook and Campbell, 1979). Researchers in multicultural education have often failed to describe programs adequately, thus confounding the construct validity of their studies. Even in the ways that variables are operationalized there are other threats to what Walberg (1984) has called the "analytical validity" of research. Analytical validity points to problems in compositing variables, exemplified by "stereotyping complex patterns of basic variables into a single variable or typology" (Walberg, 1984, p. 393). For example, race, ethnicity, gender, and social class are nominal- and ordinal-level variables. Ethnicity and race often must be dichotomized, and dummy variables created, in order to be used in regression models: that is, operational definitions of variables may entail the aggregation of ethnic groups into black versus nonblack, or Hispanic versus non-Hispanic. The reason may be that each separate racial or ethnic group lacks sufficient representation in the sample size, which introduces the possibility of inflated error terms and standard errors. (As I have heard social scientists say, you can call it anthropology when the number of independent variables is greater than the sample size.) Small sample sizes also result in low statistical power, a bias that can be corrected in the calculation of effect sizes.

External validity concerns the generalizability of findings to other groups, settings, and times. The generalizability of quantitative findings in multicultural education studies may be seriously confounded. Selection of experimental and control groups for multicultural education research may be one of the biggest problems. Randomization of subjects has been the canon of sampling strategies but may mask results needed for observing differences in multicultural research. Program evaluators must be aware of the drawbacks of using nonequivalent control groups (Cook and Campbell, 1979). When calculating effect sizes for meta-analysis, the researcher must be explicit in selecting an approach for combining between- and within-group variance. If status groups are assigned to experimental groups only, comparisons may be invalid. One issue that may be addressed by meta-analysis is the optimum distribution of ethnicity, gender, disability, and social-class characteristics in the classroom and in the school, a dilemma studied by Coleman (1990).

In analyzing results of individual studies, it is apparent that if analysis-of-variance (ANOVA) techniques have been used, tests for interactions may have assessed three or four factors—ethnicity, race, gender, and social class. If this approach is not taken, multiple statistical tests must be done, introducing Type I error and false positive findings. Independent tests must be evaluated carefully, to make sure that the alpha levels of the tests are correct and unbiased. Finally, as resistant as evaluators have been to the use of aptitude-treatment interaction studies, this design may be needed to study levels of educational treatment. An example can be found in the application of learning-styles research to the analysis of cross-cultural differences in students (Dunn, Gemake, Jalali, and Zenhausern, 1990). In this research, individual learning preferences are used to prescribe instructional strategies with a multidimensional learning-styles model consisting of twenty-one elements, as in the study of the effects of matching and mismatching students' math achievement when preferences for analytical, sequential instruction versus global, holistic strategies are diagnosed and taken into account (Dunn, Bruno, Sklar, and Beaudry, 1990). Previous research has used repeated-measures ANOVA models to match and mismatch learners according to strongest learning preference; successful outcomes would show interactions on a within-subjects variable.

Examples of Meta-Analyses

Effects of Examiner Familiarity on Test Performance. One of the best examples of meta-analysis probing the effects of racial/ethnic factors that I have located is the study of Fuchs and Fuchs (1989), in which the authors investigated the context of test taking and its effects on examinees' test scores: "Effect sizes were derived by determining the mean difference between the examinees' scores in familiar and unfamiliar examiner conditions and dividing this difference by the standard deviation of examinees' scores in the unfamiliar condition" (p. 305). They found that Hispanic and black students scored significantly higher with familiar examiners; Caucasian students showed no such interaction effects. The interpretation of these results was tentative, however, given the threat to internal and external validity. The authors felt that the racial/ethnic variable might have been confounded with social class or socioeconomic status of students. As for external validity, there were only fourteen studies in the sample. In addition, generalizability was constrained because most of the examinees were from early childhood education settings. (The possible consequences of these findings are chilling, since assignment to special education was the purpose of the testing programs.)

Bilingual Education. The motivation for the study by Willig (1985) was a series of contradictory literature reviews. In particular, a report from the U.S. Department of Education, by Baker and DeKantor (1981), called the evidence for supporting bilingual education very weak and recommended cutbacks in this area. This review was narrative and theoretical, making selected observations of the twenty-eight studies in the sample. Willig's meta-analysis was a partial replication of Baker and deKantor. After the total sample of studies was examined, five of them were found to be inadequate for use in meta-analysis. The results of the meta-analysis indicated that "when statistical controls for methodological inadequacies were employed, participation in bilingual education programs produced small to moderate differences favoring bilingual education for tests of reading, language skills, mathematics, and total achievement when the tests were in English, and for reading, language, mathematics, writing, social studies, listening comprehension, and attitudes towards school or self when administered in other languages" (Willig, 1985, p. 269).

Two major problems in the research on bilingual education were that program mechanisms were very poorly described and research methodologies were often weak, making any strong judgments of the findings in bilingual education tentative. Even so, Baker (1987) engaged Willig in a bitter debate, arguing that meta-analysis was inappropriate to this literature because "(a) inappropriate statistics were applied to the data, (b) the bilingual education treatment was confounded with other treatments in several of the studies reviewed, and (c) the studies reviewed were not sufficiently homogeneous to support a meta-analysis" (Baker, 1987, p. 351). This meta-analysis of bilingual education may foreshadow issues for future meta-analyses of multicultural education.

Synthesizing Qualitative Research

What are the potential contributions of qualitative evaluation? Much of the research conducted in the field of multicultural education has been based on qualitative methods: interviews, observations, teachers' narrative accounts, and ethnographic approaches, by Rist (1970), Ogbu (1978), LeCompte (1978), and Paley (1979), to name a few. Lather (1986) argues very poignantly that researchers must be conscious of the emancipatory power of knowledge, especially as it sensitizes individuals and groups "to their own actions and situations in the world" (p. 257). This perspective accepts that there is no value-free research or neutral education; therefore, evaluation research must develop methods for empowering participants with knowledge gained from evaluation; attempt to include reciprocity, or mutual exchange of knowledge, between the evaluator and the evaluated during evaluations; and include multiple data sources, methods, and theories to facilitate systematic reflexivity of data with a priori theory and aid in the task of deriving change-enhancing theory. This kind of "research as praxis" (Lather, 1986) is also referred to by Grant and Sleeter (1986) as education that is multicultural and social reconstructionist.

The integration of quantitative and qualitative studies has been addressed by Light and Pillemer (1984), and a specific discussion of integrative review techniques for qualitative research can be found in Noblit and Hare's concept of "meta-ethnography," which presents explicit methods for conducting "comparative textual analysis of published field studies" (Noblit and Hare, 1988, p. 5). Recently the phrase *multivocal literatures* was used to describe an approach to synthesizing case-study research (Ogawa and Malen, 1991). The phrase captures the essence of this discussion about synthesis of the research on multicultural education. There is an obvious analogy to the attempts of meta-analysis to provide a means of reducing the volume of research, with varied and often competing interpretations. As a new technique, meta-ethnography has great potential to establish a method for more inclusive interpretation, translation, and explanation of qualitative research results across studies. Just such imaginative syntheses of qualitative and quantitative research may be needed to overcome the limitations of meta-analysis or narrative reviews alone.

Conclusion

Program evaluation must take notice of the changes in our society and begin to respond to the social issues represented by multicultural education. Hate crimes and ethnic strife are reported on the front pages of newspapers and in the courts and the schools, as well as all around the world. In education, much of what we know about negative racial prejudice, biases in testing, culturally biased instructional materials, and teacher effects remains part of the hidden curriculum. Multicultural awareness and education have equal relevance for health care, business, and industry as these sectors of society cope with the shifting patterns of a culturally diverse work force.

We must continue to use such tools as research synthesis to improve program theory and strengthen the design and evaluation of the next generation of social service programs. Mention has been made of using groups of evaluators to conduct meta-analyses (Walberg, 1985). For investigation of multicultural education, it is imperative to bring together research teams that reflect cultural diversity and language differences. An example is Slaughter's description (1991) of the involvement of language-different stakeholders in cross-cultural evaluation teams. We must address insensitivity to cultural diversity in order to elevate the dialogue and critique of programs. We must seek to strengthen inferences, by replication and through Campbell's advocacy (1984) of a "contagious" model of cross-validation of programs.

One of the most difficult issues confronting evaluation researchers is the notion of validity. With all its constituent definitions and connotations, validity is one of the touchstones of design and analysis. Cultural diversity has put a distinctive cast on the notion of validity. Especially in the field of education, the variables of race, gender, ethnicity, and social class will continue to be important considerations in sampling and selection bias. What we gain in terms of more valid, generalizable findings we may sacrifice in terms of the expressive content of these variables.

What has been presented in this chapter provides a glimpse of the enormity and complexity that multicultural education implies. What multicultural education means to minority issues has everything to do with how program design, methodology, and evaluation combine and recombine with social justice—a challenging agenda for change.

References

Abrami, P., Cohen, P., and d'Appollonia, S. "Implementation Problems in Meta-analysis." *Review of Educational Research,* 1988, *58,* 151–180.

Allport, G. *The Nature of Prejudice.* (2nd ed.) New York: Doubleday, 1958.

Anyon, J. "Social Class and the Hidden Curriculum of Work." In H. Giroux, A. Penna, and W. Pinar (eds.), *Curriculum and Instruction.* Berkeley, Calif.: McCutchan, 1981.

Baker, G. "Multicultural Training for Teacher Education." *Journal of Teacher Education,* 1973, *24,* 306–308.

Baker, K. "Comment on Willig's 'A Meta-analysis of Selected Studies in the Effectiveness of Bilingual Education.'" *Review of Educational Research,* 1987, *57,* 351–362.

Baker, K., and DeKantor, A. "Effectiveness of Bilingual Education: A Review of the Literature." Final draft report. Washington, D.C.: Office of Technical and Analytic Systems, U.S. Department of Education, 1981.

Banks, J. *Multiethnic Education: Theory and Practice.* Needham Heights, Mass.: Allyn & Bacon, 1988.

Barrington, B., and Hendricks, B. "Differentiating Characteristics of High School Graduates, Dropouts, and Nongraduates." *Journal of Educational Research,* 1989, *82,* 309–316.

Baty, R. *Re-educating Teachers for Cultural Awareness.* New York: Praeger, 1972.

Beaudry, J. "Pluralistic Pedagogy: Evaluation of a Program to Recruit Minorities into the Teaching Profession." Paper presented at the annual meeting of the American Educational Research Association, Boston, 1990.

Bennett, K., and LeCompte, M. *The Way Schools Work: A Sociological Analysis of Education.* White Plains, N.Y.: Longman, 1990.

Bryk, A., and Thum, Y. "The Effects of High School Organization on Dropping Out: An Exploratory Investigation." *American Educational Research Journal,* 1989, *26,* 353–384.

Campbell, D. "Can We Be Scientific in Applied Social Science?" In R. Connor, D. Altman, and H. Preskill (eds.), *Evaluation Studies Review Annual.* Newbury Park, Calif.: Sage, 1984.

Campbell, J. "American Ethnic Groups Supply New Evidence to Socialization Differences Between Males and Females in Mathematics." Paper presented at the annual meeting of the American Educational Research Association, San Francisco, March 1989.

Carlberg, C., and Walberg, H. "Techniques of Research Synthesis." *Journal of Special Education,* 1984, *18,* 11–26.

Coleangelo, N., Dustin, D., and Foxley, C. *Multicultural Nonsexist Education.* Dubuque, Iowa: Kendall/Hunt, 1985.

Coleman, J. *Equality and Achievement in Education.* Boulder, Colo.: Westview Press, 1990.

Coleman, J., Campbell, E., Hobson, C., McPartland, J., Mood, A., Weinfeld, F., and York, R. *Equality of Educational Opportunity.* Washington, D.C.: U.S. Government Printing Office, 1966.

Contreras, A. "Multicultural Attitudes and Knowledge of Education Students at Indiana University." Paper presented at the annual meeting of the American Educational Research Association, New Orleans, April 1988.

Cook, T., and Campbell, D. *Quasi-Experimentation: Design and Analysis Issues for Research.* Skokie, Ill.: Rand McNally, 1979.

Cooper, H. *Integrating Research: A Guide for Literature Reviews.* Newbury Park, Calif.: Sage, 1989.

Darling-Hammond, L. "Teachers and Teaching: Signs of a Changing Profession." In R. Houston (ed.), *Handbook of Research in Teacher Education.* New York: Macmillan, 1989.

Dewey, J. *Experience and Education.* New York: Collier Books, 1938.

Dunn, R., Bruno, J., Sklar, R., and Beaudry, J. "The Effects of Matching and Mismatching Minority Developmental College Students' Hemispheric Preferences on Mathematics Test Scores." *Journal of Educational Research,* 1990, *83,* 283–288.

Dunn, R., Gemake, J., Jalali, F., and Zenhausern, R. "Cross-Cultural Differences in Learning Styles of Elementary-Age Students from Four Ethnic Backgrounds." *Journal of Multicultural Counseling and Development,* 1990, *18,* 68–91.

Fuchs, D., and Fuchs, L. "Effects of Examiner Familiarity on Black, Caucasian, and Hispanic Children: A Meta-analysis." *Exceptional Children,* 1989, *55,* 303–308.

Gay, G. "Multiethnic Education: Historical Developments and Future Prospects." *Phi Delta Kappan,* 1983, *64,* 560–563.

Gill, S., and Zimmerman, N. "Racial/Ethnic and Gender Bias in the Courts: A Stakeholder-Focused Approach." *Evaluation Practice,* 1990, *11,* 103–108.

Giroux, H. "Hegemony, Resistance, and the Paradox of Educational Reform." In H. Giroux, A. Penna, and W. Pinar (eds.), *Curriculum and Instruction.* Berkeley, Calif.: McCutchan, 1981.

Glass, G., McGaw, B., and Smith, M. "Meta-analysis in Social Research." Newbury Park, Calif.: Sage, 1981.

Grant, C. "Education That Is Multicultural and Teacher Preparation: An Examination from the Perspective of Preservice Students." *Journal of Educational Research,* 1981, *75,* 95–99.

Grant, C., and Grant, G. "Staff Development and Education That Is Multicultural: A Study of an Inservice Institute for Teachers and Principals." *British Journal of Inservice Education,* 1985, *2,* 6–18.

Grant, C., and Secada, W. "Preparing Teachers for Diversity." In R. Houston (ed.), *Handbook of Research in Teacher Education.* New York: Macmillan, 1989.

Grant, C., and Sleeter, C. "Race, Class, and Gender in Education Research: An Argument for Integrative Analysis." *Review of Educational Research,* 1986, *56,* 195–211.

Grant, C., and Sleeter, C. *Turning on Learning: Five Approaches for Multicultural Teaching for Race, Class, Gender, and Disability.* Columbus, Ohio: Merrill, 1989.

Haertel, G., and Walberg, H. "Assessing Social-Psychological Classroom Environments." In K. Conrad and C. Roberts-Gray (eds.), *Evaluating Program Environments.* New Directions for Program Evaluation, no. 40. San Francisco: Jossey-Bass, 1988.

Hedges, L., and Olkin, I. *Statistical Methods for Meta-analysis.* Orlando, Fla.: Academic Press, 1985.

Hennington, M. "Effect of Intensive Multicultural Nonsexist Instruction on Secondary Student Teachers." *Education Research Quarterly,* 1981, *6,* 65–75.

House, E. "Evaluation and Social Justice." In M. McLaughlin and D. Phillips (eds.), *Evaluation and Education at Quarter Century: Ninetieth Yearbook of the National Society for the Study of Education.* Chicago: University of Chicago Press, 1991.

Hunter, J., Schmidt, F., and Jackson, G. *Meta-analysis: Cumulating Research Findings Across Studies.* Newbury Park, Calif.: Sage, 1991.

Institute for Educational Leadership. *School Boards: Strengthening Grass-Roots Leadership.* Washington, D.C.: Institute for Educational Leadership, 1986.

Klassen, F., and Gollnick, D. *Pluralism and the American Teacher: Issues and Case Studies.* Washington, D.C.: Ethnic Heritage Center for Teacher Education, American Association of Colleges of Teacher Education, 1977.

Ladson-Billings, G. "Beyond Multicultural Illiteracy." *Journal of Negro Education,* 1991, *60,* 147–157.

Larke, P., and McJamerson, E. "Cultural Diversity Awareness Inventory of Preservice Teachers." Paper presented at the annual meeting of the American Educational Research Association, Boston, April 1990.

Lather, P. "Research as Praxis." *Harvard Educational Review,* 1986, *56,* 257-277.

LeCompte, M. "Learning to Work: The Hidden Curriculum of the Classroom." *Anthropology and Education Quarterly,* 1978, *9,* 23-27.

Light, R., and Pillemer, D. *Summing Up.* Cambridge, Mass.: Harvard University Press, 1984.

Mahan, J. "Native Americans as Teacher Trainers: Anatomy and Outcomes of a Cultural Immersion Project." *Journal of Equity and Leadership,* 1982, *2,* 100-110.

Miller, D. *Handbook of Research Design and Social Measurement.* Newbury Park, Calif.: Sage, 1991.

Noblit, G., and Hare, R. *Meta-ethnography: Synthesizing Qualitative Research Studies.* Newbury Park, Calif.: Sage, 1988.

Noordhoff, K., and Kleinfeld, J. "Preparing Teachers for Multicultural Classrooms: A Case Study in Rural Alaska." Paper presented at the annual meeting of the American Educational Research Association, Chicago, 1991.

Ogawa, R., and Malen, B. "Towards Rigor in Reviews of Multivocal Literatures: Applying the Exploratory Case Method." *Review of Educational Research,* 1991, *61,* 265-286.

Ogbu, J. *Minority Status and Caste: The American System in Cross-cultural Perspective.* San Diego, Calif.: Academic Press, 1978.

O'Sullivan, R. "Using a Developmental Framework to Design an Evaluation Guide for Three Statewide Georgia Programs for High-Risk Students." Paper presented at the annual meeting of the American Evaluation Association, Washington, D.C., 1990.

Pai, Y. *Cultural Foundations of Education.* New York: Macmillan, 1990.

Paley, V. *White Teacher.* Cambridge, Mass.: Harvard University Press, 1979.

Pallas, A., Natriello, G., and McDill, E. "The Changing Nature of the Disadvantaged Population: Current Dimensions and Future Trends." *Educational Researcher,* 1989, *18,* 16-22.

Rist, R. "Student Social Class and Teacher Expectations: The Self-Fulfilling Prophecy in Ghetto Education." *Harvard Educational Review,* 1970, *40,* 411-451.

Rosenthal, R. *Meta-analytic Procedures for Social Research.* Newbury Park, Calif.: Sage, 1984.

Rothenburg, P. *Racism and Sexism.* New York: St. Martin's Press, 1988.

Slaughter, H. "The Participation of Cultural Informants on Bilingual and Cross-cultural Evaluation Teams." *Evaluation Practice,* 1991, *12,* 149-157.

Slavin, R. "Ability Grouping and Student Achievement in Elementary Schools: A Best-Evidence Synthesis." *Review of Educational Research,* 1987, *57,* 293-337.

Sleeter, C. "A Need for Research on Preservice Teacher Education for Mainstreaming and Multicultural Education." *Journal of Equity and Leadership,* 1985, *5,* 205-215.

Sleeter, C., and Grant, C. "An Analysis of Multicultural Education in the United States." *Harvard Educational Review,* 1987, *57,* 412-444.

Walberg, H. "Quantification Reconsidered." In E. W. Gordon (ed.), *Review on Research in Education.* Washington, D.C.: American Educational Research Association, 1984.

Walberg, H. "Syntheses of Research on Teaching." In M. Wittrock (ed.), *Handbook of Research on Teaching.* New York: Macmillan, 1985.

Warshaw, C., Olson, J., and Beaudry, J. "Implications of Meyer and Scott's Theory of Institutional Environments for the Implementation of Cummins' Framework for the Empowerment of Students of Bilingual Kindergartens." Unpublished paper, National Clearinghouse for Bilingual Education, abstracted in *Resources in Education,* April 1991. (BEO 179 919)

Washington, V. "Impact of Antiracism/Multicultural Education Training on Elementary Teachers' Attitudes and Classroom Behavior." *Elementary School Journal,* 1981, *81,* 186-192.

Wayson, W. "Multicultural Education Among Seniors in the College of Education at Ohio State University." Paper presented at the annual meeting of the American Educational Research Association, New Orleans, April 1988.

Weiss, C. "Evaluation Research in the Political Context: Sixteen Years and Four Administrations Later." In M. McLaughlin and D. Phillips (eds.), *Evaluation and Education at Quarter Century: Ninetieth Yearbook of the National Society for the Study of Education.* Chicago: University of Chicago Press, 1991.

Willig, A. "A Meta-analysis of Selected Studies on the Effectiveness of Bilingual Education." *Review of Educational Research,* 1985, *55,* 269–317.

Willis, S. "The Inclusive Curriculum: Multicultural Content Increasingly a School Goal." *ASCD Update,* 1990, *32,* p. 1.

JEFFREY S. BEAUDRY is assistant professor in the Division of Administrative and Instructional Leadership, School of Education and Human Services, St. John's University, Jamaica, New York.

INDEX

Abrahams, R. D., 50
Abrami, P., 79
Activities, educational, 22
Affirmations, 39
African American: accurate evaluation, 64-65; at-risk students, 45; demographics of households, 59; developmental evaluation, 28; Making a Difference Is Our Business, 22; misconceptions, 59; Multicultural Education Program, 17-18; quality of education, 71; race perceptions, 59; religious values, 55; SAT scores, 41; in Texas, 8
Allen, W., 59
Allport, G. W., 57, 71-72
America: browning of, 45; in transformation, 19
American Indians, Multicultural Education Program: 17-18; On Eagle's Wings, 22. *See also* Native Americans
Analysis of covariance (ANCOVA), 62
ANCOVA. *See* Analysis of covariance
Anyon, J., 71
Aronowitz, S., 49
Asian: at-risk students, 45; limited English proficiency, 49; SAT scores, 51
Assertions, 39
Assumptions, program, 28
At-risk: educational term, 7-8, 11; students in Texas, 5, 7; students in U.S., 45; technical definition, 7
Attendance policy, Texas, 5

Baizerman, M., 5, 7
Baker, K., 73, 80, 81
Banks, J., 72-73
Banton, A., 58
Barriers: breaking down, 25; choice of words, 23, 69; different world view, 23-24; evaluation implications, 24-25; getting unstuck, 25; to multicultural programs, 22-25; white institutional power, 24
Barrington, B., 74
Bartel, N. R., 48
Baty, R., 74
Baugh, J., 48

Beaudry, J. S., 69-70, 75, 80
Bennett, K., 73
Biases: cultural, 38; initial, 40-41
Bickman, L., 38, 56
Bigelow Foundation. *See* F. R. Bigelow Foundation
Bilingual education, 80-81
Bishop, A. H., 13
Black Americans, 71. *See also* African American
Bowles, S., 49
Boykin, A. W., 58, 60
Briggs, C. L., 50
Bronfenbrenner, U., 47
Brown v. Board of Education, 71
Bruner, J., 47
Bruno, J., 80
Bryden, D. N., 48
Bryk, A., 57, 74
Buber, M., 10
Buberian Other, 13
Bush, President George, 5
Bush Foundation, The, 21

Cambodians: developmental evaluation, 28; Multicultural Education Program, 17; New Year celebration, 22
Campbell, D., 79, 82
Campbell, E., 71
Campbell, J., 71
Carlberg, C., 78
Carver, R. P., 62
CETA, 62
Changes, in everyday lives, 8
Chen, H. T., 38, 40, 56-57
Chicanos, social programs, 71. *See also* Hispanic Americans
Civil Rights Act, 71
Claims: document, 29; program, 28; sample SDS statement, 30
Classical methods, evaluation, 10
CLAST. *See* College-Level Academic Skills Test
Cognition, and culture, 47-48
Cohen, P., 79
Colangelo, N., 73
Cole, M., 47

ORDERING INFORMATION

NEW DIRECTIONS FOR PROGRAM EVALUATION is a series of paperback books that presents the latest techniques and procedures for conducting useful evaluation studies of all types of programs. Books in the series are published quarterly in Fall, Winter, Spring, and Summer and are available for purchase by subscription as well as by single copy.

SUBSCRIPTIONS for 1992 cost $48.00 for individuals (a savings of 20 percent over single-copy prices) and $70.00 for institutions, agencies, and libraries. Please do not send institutional checks for personal subscriptions. Standing orders are accepted.

SINGLE COPIES cost $15.95 when payment accompanies order. (California, New Jersey, New York, and Washington, D.C., residents please include appropriate sales tax.) Billed orders will be charged postage and handling.

DISCOUNTS FOR QUANTITY ORDERS are available. Please write to the address below for information.

ALL ORDERS must include either the name of an individual or an official purchase order number. Please submit your order as follows:
   Subscriptions: specify series and year subscription is to begin
   Single copies: include individual title code (such as PE1)

MAIL ALL ORDERS TO:
   Jossey-Bass Publishers
   350 Sansome Street
   San Francisco, California 94104

FOR SALES OUTSIDE OF THE UNITED STATES CONTACT:
   Maxwell Macmillan International Publishing Group
   866 Third Avenue
   New York, New York 10022

OTHER TITLES AVAILABLE IN THE
NEW DIRECTIONS FOR PROGRAM EVALUATION SERIES
Nick L. Smith, *Editor-in-Chief*